Paul Hardy

The Pocket Essential

FILMING ON A MICROBUDGET

www.pocketessentials.com

First published in Great Britain 2001 by Pocket Essentials, 18 Coleswood Road,
Harpenden, Herts, AL5 1EQ

Distributed in the USA by Trafalgar Square Publishing, PO Box 257, Howe Hill
Road, North Pomfret, Vermont 05053

A CIP catalogue record for this book is available from the British Library.

ISBN 1-903047-48-X

9 8 7 6 5 4 3 2 1

Book typeset by Pdunk
Printed and bound by Cox & Wyman

for my Grandmother

Acknowledgements

Andy Brooks, Dominic Day, Jason Fairley, Anne Forgan, Sandra Hall, Den Hands, Andy McGeechan, Mike Roberts, Matthew Taylor, Nerina Villa, Tom Wright - thanks for helping me learn how to do all this stuff or for correcting me while I was writing. And huge thanks to everyone at the Depot Studios in Coventry and Vivid in Birmingham without whom I wouldn't be able to make films at all.

CONTENTS

Introduction

Very few people make short films simply to make short films. It's a training ground, an apprenticeship, a way of breaking the Catch-22 of the film industry: you're not allowed to make anything until you've already made something. And what's more, it doesn't require the potentially destructive investment of time, effort and money that making a feature requires. With a good short film to your name, screened on television or shown at an appropriate film festival or distributed on the Internet or sent to the right producer, you might get offered that dream job directing a film - or find that doors suddenly start to swing open when you try to get your own feature off the ground. Or you might not. But even if the film gets nowhere it will have given you valuable experience, and taught you enough of what not to do so that the next one is better.

So you make your film on a microbudget. 'Microbudget' means no money, or very little. But the term is misleading. A ten-minute film budgeted for £50 might well cost £500, or £10,000, or £50,000 if every last item is paid for at the going rate. Ways of achieving this are many and varied; the only common thread with most of the films I've seen made on microbudgets is that everyone exploited what resources they had as ruthlessly as they could, and never acknowledged the word 'impossible' if they could come up with an original way of doing something. Producing a microbudget film requires a certain attitude as much as anything. Nothing is impossible, as long as you're tenacious (or bloody-minded) and imaginative (or desperate) enough.

One thing that I'm assuming is that you'll be shooting on video. Shooting on film is certainly not impossible to do on a microbudget, and there are myriad stories of people who managed to do it on next to no money, but few of us are lucky enough to have the right set of contacts and knowledge to be able to accomplish all this. Good, near-broadcast quality video is so easily and widely available these days that your first attempts at film-making are best made on a medium which is easier to learn and more forgiving of mistakes.

At the most basic, all you need to make a film is a VHS video camera and a video recorder - you film something with the camera, then edit by re-recording the shots, in whatever order you want, onto a tape in the VCR. And if you buy some cheap leads and adapters, you can transfer music onto the tape as well. And if your income is higher, you can buy a home computer on which to edit your film, and a tiny DV camera that can take footage you'd be hard-pressed to distinguish from professional broadcast quality video. The technology of film production has never been so widely available.

Which leaves one thing which can't be improved by technology: you, the film maker. The one talent you need is the ability to imagine a series of images (not necessarily with dialogue or even with sound) that tell a story. Everything else can be learnt by observation and experience. You should watch as many films (in the cinema) and as much television (even the ads) as you can, and with a critical eye. And you must make films. If you can't get into film school or can't afford it or just don't have the time, you have to jump in and learn the job by doing it. This book will help you by showing the process by which short films are made, and giving you the information you need to make the best film you can with the resources you have available; you still have to go out and do the work, and you'll still make mistakes but, hopefully, the way will be a little smoother.

Having made many of these mistakes myself, I wouldn't want you to repeat them without being warned…

Note: Film-making is full of all kinds of weird jargon, so I have added an extensive glossary at the back of this book to help you out.

Development

The Idea

Getting an idea for a film is more or less your own business. For every person, the process is different. But once you've got an idea, you need to subject it to a couple of very tough questions before you actually turn it into a film.

• **Is It The Right Length?** - Short films can be anything from a few seconds to 40 minutes or so. The longer the film, the more difficult it's going to be to make; if your story is running long, it may be worth considering using it to build an idea for a feature film. Longer fictional shorts are very difficult to find distribution for. Ten minutes is commonly considered an appropriate length. Many short film schemes run by television companies require this, and cinema distributors of short films stipulate this as the maximum. Ten minutes will allow you to go into some depth with an idea, and is a good benchmark to set yourself. There is also something to be said for making a very short film of 60-90 seconds; while this may not seem like much, bear in mind that television commercials are often shorter and yet are capable of telling a perfectly good story. It's an excellent way to learn a very efficient approach to storytelling which will pay off when you make longer films.

• **Do I Have The Resources To Do This?** - If your idea concerns space aliens battling Roman soldiers upon the bloody fields of the Somme, then the answer is probably no. If it involves the titanic struggles of your child to throw a ball through a hoop, then the answer is probably yes. Take a look at the idea and work out if you can do it. That includes the time you have to do it. Are you completely free? Do you have holiday time coming up? Can you only shoot on weekends?

Or you can work the other way round. Make a list of all the things, people or places that you could use to make a film, and see if that sparks your imagination to come up with an idea. Robert Rodriguez (*El Mariachi*, *Desperado*, *The Faculty*) made a short film called *Bedhead* with his brothers and sisters as performers, the family house as a location, and only what was already available in the house for props. It went on to win multiple awards.

With imagination, a good telephone manner and a great deal of persistence, you can extend the possibilities enormously. It's remarkable what you can get if you simply ask; one friend of mine was able to get hold of a helicopter for free without much trouble. If you live in a place which isn't used to film shoots, you're much more likely to be successful than you are if you live somewhere that entertains them on a regular basis. Most people have a fascination with film and television productions which makes them willing to assist you simply for the pleasure of observing a film being made; but then again, some people don't. It depends entirely upon who you talk to at any given time. But treat people nicely and with respect, and you'll be amazed at how far they're willing to go for you.

The only sure way to get a sense for the possibilities and limitations of filming on a microbudget is experience. I strongly recommend that you make your first film with what's available at hand or for a low price, on the cheapest video format available to you (VHS is very good for this). Use it to experiment and get a feel for the process; there's no need to even show your first few attempts to anyone if you feel you might be embarrassed by them. They're just for you, so you can find out how to make films. Simply getting the hang of how to use a camera and how to edit shots together is worth taking the time over. And then, with each film you make, try and set yourself more challenging things to do. Stretch your capabilities and force yourself to learn by doing.

Script & Structure

Story Structure

Writers often like to give the impression that when an idea struck them, it came fully-formed and ready to be typed out and rushed to the printers immediately. Films often show the process of writing a screenplay as a matter of putting paper in a typewriter and banging away at the keyboard until all the pages are filled.

This, unfortunately, is a lie. The actual process of writing involves a lot of hard work, dead ends, and rewriting. Inspiration isn't enough. You have to find a way of structuring your idea into a story. Story structure is nothing to be frightened of; it lurks beneath the surface of every story you've ever heard or seen, and normally goes unnoticed - unless you know what you're looking for. Structure works on the basis of cycles of rising action; the tension in the story mounts until something major happens, then ebbs for a quiet moment and builds up again to another major event which tops the first; and repeat until the end of the story, the last act ending on another major scene which tops anything that has gone before. Each of these build-ups and major scenes at the end is called an act. Feature films usually have three or four, while short films might only have one, and quite often, that will be a single scene - but they will follow this pattern even within that one scene.

The simplest structure is the same as that of a joke. Set-up and punchline. Here's an example, from Jeff Stark's short film, *Desserts*: A man walks along an empty beach. He finds an exquisite cake lying upon the sand. He picks it up; sniffs it; decides it's okay. He eats it. The hook inside snags into his mouth, and the line attached to it pulls him out into the ocean. Set-up and punchline. It may seem absolutely bloody obvious, but think about what would happen to the joke if it weren't properly set up, or the punchline (known more generally as the 'pay-off') wasn't completely shown: the joke wouldn't be funny.

The trick is to give the audience what they want, but not in the way they are expecting. As soon as we see that cake on the sand, we're expecting something to happen, and it does, but it's so strange and beyond what we could have expected that we react to it. This doesn't just work for comedy. If the man had picked up the cake and bitten into it only to find a telephone number written on a scrap of paper buried in the cream, it wouldn't be funny, but it would be intriguing. Who on earth would leave a cream cake with a telephone number in it on a beach? It's also an example of how the pay-off of a scene can become a set-up for another scene; what happens when the man calls that number? The audience will want to know. And if you don't satisfy that demand - while giving them something unexpected in the process - they're going to be disappointed.

Another way to keep things interesting is by using subtext. An example: Two people are watching television. One has control of the remote and is paying strict attention to the set. The other is talking very loudly about what they have been doing at work. The 'text' (in this case, people watching and not watching TV) is what we see and hear; the 'subtext' (the fact that these two people detest each other) is what's actually going on. We may be aware of it simply through the actors' performances or we may know these characters from before this conversation, and be well aware that every word and gesture is loaded with extra meaning.

The best principle for storytelling is: show, don't tell. We usually speak of 'telling a story,' but in film, what you should really be doing is 'showing a story.' The basic ability of a film-maker is to string together a sequence of images that tells a story - not a sequence of speeches. Changes and revelations should be, as far as possible, transmitted to the audience in a visual manner. Consider the example of *Desserts*; did the man on the beach need to get out his mobile and tell his mate that he'd found a cake on the sand and that it was really weird and that he wasn't sure if it was safe to eat or not? No. If an audience sees something for themselves, then they become more involved than if they had simply been told the same information. Of course, it's not always possible to make a film without having people speak to each other, but if the dialogue has subtext, the principle still works; if two people are talking about something innocuous but there's a deeper meaning, then the audience has to make that little bit of deduction which gets them more interested in what's happening. Something has been shown without being directly told.

Script Format

Do you need to write a properly formatted screenplay for your short film? No. What you need is a blueprint for your film which will enable you to get your ideas across to other people, and make you decide what you need for your film. In most cases, a script is the best way to do this, since most films will require a mixture of visual action and dialogue, but there's nothing to prevent you from coming up with your own system.

Properly formatted scripts (and the format is different to that of plays or TV) do have one very useful feature which will assist you in making the film: on average, a single page of formatted script equals one minute of screen time. Working out the length of your film is a matter of counting the pages, allowing for a couple of minutes' variation. It's also (according to the industry) a minimum standard of professionalism - if you send someone an unformatted script, they may file it in the bin.

These are the settings for script format (see example):
- **Slugline** All capitals. 1½" from the left edge of paper
- **Screen Description** 1½" from the left edge of paper
- **Character Name** All capitals. 3½" from left edge of paper
- **Dialogue** 2½" from left edge of paper
- **Personal Direction** 2¼" from left edge of paper
- **Effects** Right aligned. 1" from right edge of paper
- **Top and bottom margin** 1"
- **Font for everything** 12pt Courier

Some films can and should have a different blueprint. A film that is entirely visual and has no actors (particularly animation) is best designed with a storyboard. A film that is to be improvised by actors may require a list of scenes and information on the characters, rather than specific instructions on what to do and say. A film with no dialogue and no actors may simply require a shotlist. It's up to you to decide what your production needs.

Scripting Format Example:

FADE IN:

EXT. BUSY STREET - DAY

A NAKED MAN walks from a side street and plants a banner in a council flowerbed-

"SCRIPT FORMAT TUITION"

INT. WALK-IN REFRIGERATOR - NIGHT

The location has changed but the Naked Man is here still. He shivers and clings on to the banner.

> NAKED MAN
> That location thing is a slugline, okay?
> INT means Interior, EXT means Exterior,
> then you say where it is, then you say
> what time of day it is. Very important for
> lighting!

He points at a window, which shows the moon.

> NAKED MAN (CONT'D)
> (whispering)
> I'm whispering to show you that personal
> direction, in the brackets there. Don't
> overuse it! Actors don't like being told
> how to do their job. Can we go somewhere
> warm now?

EXT. ACTIVE VOLCANO - RIM - DAY

CRANE SHOT up from LAVA TRACKING IN on Naked Man as he DANCES on the blistering surface. FOCUS PULL onto banner as it falls and BLAZES into charcoal.

> NAKED MAN (CONT'D)
> Who do you think you are? The DIRECTOR? No
> camera directions!

The Naked Man bursts into flames.

> NAKED MAN (CONT'D)
> Keep paragraphs four lines or less! Read-
> ers get frightened if they see a big block
> of text.

He falls into the pit.

FADE OUT

Outline & Treatment

Before you start on the script, you need to know the story. You must write the film in outline form to get it sorted out first. Bear in mind that no one ever has to see your outline; it's a document intended for you and you alone. It doesn't need to be well formatted or even well spelt; you can write it as many times as you need to, make as many notes as required. The reason for doing this is that changes can be more easily made at this stage. Writing your story down will tell you an awful lot about how well it works; having it worked out in your head isn't enough. You don't need to describe everything; you don't need to write dialogue; just the basic, important things. My description of *Desserts*, above, is effectively an outline. If you have something more complex, you can write individual scenes on index cards and shuffle them about as necessary to help you put the plot together.

You may find yourself called upon to write a treatment, particularly if you are seeking funding of any kind. Although definitions of what it should contain vary, a treatment is always about presentation: selling your story to someone else. It has to interest the reader in a short space of time - an A4 page or less for a short film.

Directing On The Page

If you're writing a script for a director, and put in lots of camera directions, such as 'The lead character closes her eyes. Camera TRACKS BACK to reveal a WIDE SHOT of everyone standing in a line, gaping in awe. ZOOM IN on main character as she opens her eyes and STARES down the lens…' the director will ignore this blatant attempt to steal his or her job and find a completely different way to shoot the same scene. And anyway, camera directions interrupt the flow of the story. The aim is to get the reader submerged in the reading experience, not to distract them with technical information. Even if you're directing the film, you will have other collaborators, and there's no need to impress them with your knowledge of technical terms; there's every need to get them interested in the story. Write down the impression the audience should be getting, not the manner in which you intend to achieve it.

Rewriting

Once the first draft of the script is written, put it away in a drawer for a week. Then take it out and read it again. You will almost certainly find fault with it; this is a good thing, because now you have the opportunity to improve the script. You may find that you have to go back to an earlier stage in the process in order to solve the problems, but stick with it. The worst thing you can do is go into production with a script that isn't the best you can write; while a bad film can be made of a good script, it's next to impossible to make a good film out of a bad script. You might go through twenty drafts or you may need less, but you will always need to rewrite the first draft three or four times, no matter how perfect you thought it was.

Storyboarding & Shotlisting

Storyboard

A storyboard is another way of creating a blueprint for your movie, usually done once the script is completed. A storyboard looks like a comic, and that's almost precisely what it is: the film in still images. One thing you don't need is artistic ability - stick figures will do.

Although individual shots vary, there are some standard shot sizes used as a shorthand:

- **Extremely Long Shot (ELS)** Subject can be tiny in the distance or closer but with a fair amount of space around them.
- **Long Shot (LS)** Head to toe.
- **Medium Long Shot (MLS)** Head to knee.
- **Medium Shot (MS)** Head to waist. This is the 'newsreader' shot which is very common on television; it allows the subject to use their hands.
- **Medium Close-Up (MCU)** Head and shoulders.
- **Close-Up (CU)** Head.
- **Big Close-Up (BCU)** Eyes and nose.
- **Extreme Close-Up (ECU)** Eyes, or anything absurdly close.

Possible camera movements:
- **Pan** Spinning the camera left or right on a stand.
- **Tilt** Tilting the camera backward or forward so that it looks up or down.
- **Track** Physically moving the camera backwards or forwards.
- **Track Sideways/'Crab'** Physically moving the camera sideways.
- **Zoom** Using a zoom lens to get closer to or further from a subject.

What you're creating is an edit of your film before you've even shot it. It's possible to plan things in such detail so that you need make no decisions when you're editing, but that takes a great deal of experience. If you just want to have a good selection of shots to experiment with, then shoot 'coverage.' Generally, this will include:
- A **Master** shot of the entire scene from beginning to end, shot wide to get everything in.
- **Singles** on each character, covering all their actions. Try to get more

than one shot size on a character, depending on what they're doing.

• **Cutaways** Details on any physical action, like the pouring of a drink, fingers tapping etc. These may be required by the script, but shoot more, as they will be useful to conceal problems.

• **Anything else you can think of** Whatever seems like a good idea. Experiment!

Shooting coverage just by itself is, in the long run, quite a dull way to shoot a film, but it will get you started. When you have scenes where people are just talking to each other, the final edit will depend mostly on the performances you get from the actors, so decide upon a few shots to cover the whole action - but not necessarily the standard ones. You can shoot directly from above or below, move the camera around them in a circle, pan between them every time they speak - the only rule is: "Does it tell the story without getting in the way?" In scenes where it's mainly action (which doesn't necessarily mean violence), you will need to storyboard much more tightly, but should still leave yourself some options when you're editing.

Shotlisting

Once you have a finished storyboard, you can work out how many shots you need to do. And once you have that information, you can work out how many lighting set-ups you need to do, and how many shots for each one. And once you know that, you can have a rough guess at how long it will take to shoot - and a full schedule is just round the corner.

The shotlist is a tool for planning, and planning is key to getting a film made. On set, you'll probably be using the shotlist as your guide to what needs to be done (the storyboard is too bulky). Put as much information as you think necessary in it. Once you've made the list, put it into two orders: the editing order, and the likely shooting order. I find that spreadsheet programs are best for shotlisting, since they allow easier shuffling and sorting for this purpose.

Storyboard Example:

EXAMPLE STORYBOARD PAGE ONE

ELS MASTER

BOY: "FRAN! HI!"
GIRL: "JIM..."

MCU

GIRL: "YOU BASTARD!"

CU

BOY: "WHAT? WHAT
DID I DO?"

ECU OF POLAROID

GIRL: "WHO'S THIS?!!"

MLS SUPERFAST TRACK
IN ON BOY FOLLOWING
POLAROID

CONT'D. BCU, END OF
TRACK. BOY SWEATING
BOY: "IT'S YOU WITH A WIG
ON?"

17

Pre-Production

Scheduling

Film-making is a problem-solving exercise, and the key to problem solving is planning. You cannot charge blindly in and create a story with unrealistic requirements, and expect that everything will end up exactly as you envisaged. There's so much that can go wrong when you're making a film that you need to be as certain as you possibly can of what's supposed to happen. So you need to make a schedule.

There are two aspects to scheduling: the overall production, from pre-production through to distribution; and the shoot itself.

The Overall Production

You're going to need a diary. Make sure you have all the days when you're working or otherwise unavailable marked off; what's left will decide how you organise the shoot. Presuming that you already have a script, you should choose as your shoot dates a period something like three months ahead; this will give you ample time to get locations, equipment, props, cast and crew. Make it longer if your spare time is limited. A ten-minute drama will generally take between three and five days to shoot. It's best to have these in a row, and running over a weekend, but shooting on consecutive weekends is perfectly okay, bearing in mind that it might incur things like extra travel costs. Auditioning should be over and done with at least 6 weeks before the shoot; if you're dealing with professional actors, they will need to have a fair amount of prior notice that they've got the job.

After the shoot, a week or so should be left clear for recovery and to log the footage. You may want to give yourself another week to do a rough cut of the film on VHS or a cheap computer system; the main edit should take about 5 days, but it can, of course, vary. Music is usually composed after the visual side of the edit is locked down, and recording time will need to be booked for it; and then another day in the edit suite to add it to the film.

One benefit of booking everything way in advance is that you force yourself to get the film done, instead of finding yourself completing post-production in dribs and drabs over a period of months. While it's fine to experiment, letting it drag on forever is only stopping you from making your next film and learning even more.

The Shoot

Firstly, number all the scenes - give each slugline a separate number so it's easier to shuffle them about. The example on the opposite page will give you an idea of how to write up a schedule; a ten-hour day is quite normal, but remember that twelve hours is the legal maximum. Bear in mind that the wrap at the end of the day will usually take a fair amount of time in and of itself, especially if there's a lot of lighting or scenery to take down.

Schedule Example:
Schedule: "Stitched"
Friday 10 November, 2000

```
08.00    RDV:        10, Any Old Road, Coventry (see map 1)
                     Parking: Along Ave, Coventry (park nicely -
                     people live here!)

                     CREW CALL

09:00    CAST CALL:  Miles Gallant
                     John Costello

10.00    SHOOT:      EXT. DIXON'S HOUSE - DAY
13:00    LUNCH       11,12,13,14,15

14:30    RDV:        Top floor, Lea Mills Car Park (See Map 2)
                     Parking: Floor 4a, Lea Mills Car Park

                     MINIMAL CREW ONLY. Other crew to next loc. to
                     set up

                     CAST CALL:  Miles Gallant
                                 Press Pack x10
                     CAR:        Jaguar Mark X

                     SHOOT:      EXT. CAR PARK - DAY
                                 6

15:30    RDV:        Flanker & Firkin, Greyfriars Lane (Map 2)
                     Parking: Greyfriars St Car Park

                     CAST CALL:  Paul Cawley
                                 John Newton
                                 Richard Wells
                                 Anna Scholl
                                 Pub Extras x10

16:30    SHOOT:      INT. LOCAL PUB- NIGHT
                     28
18:00    WRAP
```

Unit Moves

The most time-consuming thing you can do is to move to a new location. When you make a move, allow at least an hour for everyone to get themselves over to the new location. Prepare maps and directions for everyone, even if they know the place like the back of their hands.

Catering

Food can have a serious effect on the morale of a crew; if you feed people badly, you may find them grumbling behind your back and not giving their all. If you're only using your friends, you might be able to get them to bring packed lunches or pay for their own meals, but if you're using anyone with professional experience, you're expected to provide a free breakfast and lunch. If you don't have much money, the cast and crew might forgive you for some shortcomings; a trip to a high street baker's to get sandwiches will probably be enough, or handmade rolls (even cheaper). You should have tea and coffee available at all times, or cold drinks and water if you're expecting hot weather, along with a good supply of biscuits, chocolate and snacks. Lunch should be given an hour in the schedule. In the event of absolute disaster, people are sometimes willing to work through lunch and eat food 'in the hand,' but make sure everyone agrees to this beforehand.

Call Times

Although everything depends upon when you can get into your locations, 08:00 is a basic starting point for a first crew call, with the cast called separately depending upon when they're needed. Bear in mind that the first half an hour of a day is probably going to involve lots of unloading and getting equipment into place, so a cast call an hour after the crew call is advisable, but make sure this is early enough to allow the actors a chance to get made up and changed.

Out Of Sequence Shooting

Films are shot out of sequence to make your life bearable. Imagine you have a dialogue scene in a dark, moodily lit recording studio; you want to cut back and forth between two people as they talk. But the lighting for each angle takes half an hour or more to set up; do you really want to do that every time you need to make a cut? No. You shoot everything from one angle first, and then from another angle, and so on until you've got all the little bits and pieces on your shotlist. Shoot the widest angle first, then work your way in to the closer shots. A few repetitions of the action while it's wide will act as rehearsal for the close-ups.

Otherwise, scenes are shot in the order that it's convenient to shoot them - many considerations will come into play, such as the availability of performers, locations, daylight, local requirements and so on. You may have to juggle a bit until it all makes sense.

Lighting

Lighting set-ups are the thing that will determine how long you need to stay in any one location; every time you put the camera in a substantially different place, some sort of work will be required to adjust the lighting. Only experience will give you a rough idea of how much, but you should go through your shotlist and decide which shots are to be done from which angle, and then total up the number of angles; indoor lighting set-ups will take longer (up to an hour or more sometimes), while daytime exterior set-ups may only require the placing of a reflector to bounce a little light onto someone's face - the work of a couple of minutes.

Camera

What sort of camera movement you use also makes a difference. Exterior hand-held work is the fastest, since the camera doesn't need to be 'set up' as such, just loaded onto the shoulder. The longest set-ups usually involve a track, when the camera is moving on wheels; these movements have to be rehearsed over and over to make sure that lighting is correct throughout. The same can apply if a hand-held camera has to move about a lot in a scene; the hardest thing to do is create lighting that works in any direction no matter where the camera chooses to look.

Performers

People make mistakes, especially when it involves long, complicated dialogue scenes. If you have a shot where someone has to make a simple physical action, it will usually go a lot faster than a shot with dialogue. This is nothing to do with the professionalism of actors, but simply a measure of how much more difficult a dialogue scene is; you'll want to get it right, so give them a little more time.

Using The Weekends

Bear in mind that Saturday, Sunday and public holidays present a variety of problems and opportunities separate from other days. Sunday is a good day to do a crowd scene if you're relying on friends and family, for example. Saturday on the sea front may be a difficult shoot because of the people; but Saturday in an office is great. Plan your shoots around weekends to get the most out of the peace and quiet while it's there.

Night Shoots

Sometimes you need to shoot at night, but bear in mind what time of year it is, and exactly how many hours of night you'll have. Scheduling an eight-hour night shoot of exteriors in July is difficult; doing it in January is fine, but get prepared for the weather. Lunch breaks should be scheduled as normal, but it may be wise to provide (or pay for) a hot meal instead of just sandwiches. It's best to put night shoots at the end of the schedule, since getting back to a daytime schedule requires a couple of days taken off.

Rain

This is not a great country for film-making, as far as the weather is concerned. Luckily, light rain doesn't show up on camera, and you can go on with the assistance of plastic bags on equipment and lots of umbrellas, but waiting for the heavens to clear is a familiar experience to most film-makers. On such short shoots, it's difficult to have something else available to shoot, but if you can arrange for something to do in the event of a major downpour that sets in for the whole day, do so.

Locations

The best locations are the ones you get for free, and when you have no money, you're always looking for the best location. The easiest way to accomplish this is to write a story set in whatever locations you already have access to - your home, your workplace, public spaces, and so on. Most streets, roads and highways in the United Kingdom require no permission to film, but there are some obvious restrictions for safety and security reasons - shooting in major airports, central London, or anywhere with the initials RAF in the place name presents various difficulties.

Acquiring locations that you don't already have access to is a matter of finding them, and then persuasion. Consider a couple of options for each location you need, since you can't always get the one you want most. Things to look for in a location are:

- **Relevance** Is it right for the film? Bear in mind that many locations can double for somewhere else or be made to look different with minimal set dressing.

- **Availability** Is it going to be open at the time you need? Is it going to be open long enough? Can you persuade someone to open it for you?

- **Accessibility** Is it within range of everyone who needs to get there? Are the doors/entrance big enough to get equipment and props through? Is there disabled access?

- **Location-Specific Rules** For example, hospitals will require all mobiles to be switched off, many places are non-smoking, farmers like to have gates left closed.

- **Parking** Is there parking nearby? Is there enough? How much does it cost?

- **Power** Is there electricity on site? Is it adequate to your needs? At the very least, you'll need a socket to plug a kettle into. If you're out in the middle of nowhere, take a small camping gas cooker.

- **Light** If the sun is your main light source, does it have adequate access to your location? Where will it be shining at various times during the day (take a compass with you to check)?

- **Noise** If you're recording location sound, is there a source of noise pollution nearby, such as a major road, factory, nightclub, field of excitable sheep etc? Is it noisy all day or are there quiet times? Can you live with the noise?

- **Safety** Is the location safe? What are the fire regulations? Do they require all your equipment to be PAT tested? Is there a danger of casual theft? What's the area like for personal safety?

- **Insurance** Does the location require you to have public liability insurance? Large bureaucratic organisations are keen on this.

- **Water** Will always be required for drinking and cleaning. If you're out in the country, it's better to take water with you than rely on a standpipe.

- **Facilities** Are there sufficient toilets nearby? What are they like? If you're out in the middle of nowhere, will people mind going behind the bushes, or is it wiser to shoot near a country pub? If you're using facilities not associated with the location itself, make sure you've arranged it beforehand.

- **Changing** If your actors need to change costumes, is there somewhere private they can do this?

- **Backstage Stuff** Your make-up artist will need somewhere to work, equipment will have to be put somewhere when it's not it use, actors like to have somewhere to hang around between takes (often called a 'green room'). Remember to take some foldaway chairs with you.

- **Communications** Is there mobile coverage? Is there a working phone box nearby? In the event of an emergency, you need to be able to dial 999.
- **Events** Check that there's nothing going on during the shoot. A location may be quiet on recce, but could be the site of anything from a carnival to a funeral during the shoot.
- **Sensitivity** If your production contains material which people in the vicinity might find offensive - e.g. lots of swearing next to an old people's home, demonic rites next to a little country church, racist characters spouting off next to a mosque - you should consider things very carefully. Some things can be worked out - the racist character might be part of a film that is anti-racist, and the mosque may well approve if they're approached in the right way - but some things can't. The only rule is: be considerate.
- **Weather Refuge** Is there somewhere people can run to if it really starts pouring down? Somewhere tea and coffee can be made?
- **Proximity** How near is the location to other potential locations? It will save an enormous amount of time if you can keep your locations within a small area. For example, if you have an office scene and an alley scene to shoot, and have found the office, check the streets nearby for suitable alleys.

Some of this you can find out on a first look; some will require you to ask the owner; some will only turn up on a more detailed recce. Persuading someone to let you use their property is better learnt than taught, but here are a few tips:

- Individuals are better than organisations. If the owner is a person whom you can actually talk to - the owner of a small shop, for example - it's much easier to establish a rapport.
- Establishing that rapport can be aided by: satisfying any curiosity they may have about film shoots, listening with interest when they speak about their work, being considerate and reassuring them about any concerns they may express. If they want to observe the shoot or be an extra (and if it's possible), let them.
- With large organisations, you need to speak to the PR department (unless you have any other contacts). As long as you're not doing anything that will make them look bad, they will often allow you in. Having some local press coverage will certainly help. What you can get depends enormously on who you talk to. People at ground level are sometimes more sympathetic than people in a distant faceless office; but if you don't ask, you'll never get anywhere.
- Give a reasonable amount of advance warning; several weeks at the least. Trying to find a location to shoot something the next day can be very difficult.

• If you have no money, let them know; they'll be doubly annoyed if they feel they've been led to expect a payment when none was forthcoming.

Once you have found all your locations, check them out in detail. This is called a 'recce,' and on a short film can be done in a day. Day-to-day familiarity won't necessarily give you all the information you need; check out things like power supply and safety regulations. Never assume. If you're employing crew members, bring them along (lighting cameraman, AD and design people in particular). Their experience will help you to find out potential problems and the sort of things you'll need to bring with you.

While on location, be as considerate as possible. Any rubbish you create should be cleaned up and removed; any damage you make should be paid for. Have a member of crew responsible for fielding inquiries; this is often useful as a delaying tactic in the event of a confrontational person coming along. If you're out in public, you might find yourself needing a few people to keep pedestrians under control; areas in which you shoot can be 'locked off' for brief periods of time, but pedestrians should not be held back for too long; let them go between takes, then lock off again. Be polite if you're doing this, even if people just push past you and walk through anyway.

After the shoot, be sure to send the owners a nice letter thanking them for everything, and a VHS copy if your budget stretches that far; put the relevant name in the 'thank you' section of the credits.

Casting

The easiest thing to do is cast your friends and family. The benefits include the fact that they're free, and prepared to go out on a limb for you. But, more than likely, they are not very good actors. Even if they are, bear in mind that although the idea of making a film sounds glamorous, the reality may involve standing in a wet field in January pretending it's July. Making a film is one good way of losing all your friends, if you're not careful. If you do have a talented friend or relative, then by all means use them. But on the whole, friends and family are best employed as extras, crowds, dead bodies, zombies etc. - anything that needs a warm body but not acting ability.

Actors are surprisingly easy to find and employ, whether they be drama students looking for experience, or professional actors between jobs. Something that amazed me when I started making films was the degree to which actors were willing to work for expenses on small productions halfway up the country. Most actors are in exactly the same position as the film-maker looking to employ them - they need to be seen. And many actors who would seem to have no such need are willing to work for little or nothing if they like the script or trust you.

But you must treat your actors with the respect that you would hope to receive yourself. Simply because they're willing to work for free is no reason to exploit them. If you cannot pay someone a fee, you must still pay them expenses - travel, food and accommodation. This doesn't mean you have to put them up in a four star hotel and have a chef flown in, but putting someone out of pocket when they're giving up their time for free is nothing short of an insult. You may be able to satisfy the accommodation requirement with a sofa, a pillow and a blanket - but a spare bed is better. Another thing that actors appreciate is a VHS copy of the film when it's done. Treat your actors right, and they'll repay you for it on the screen.

The process of finding actors takes a little time and effort, but is worth it. Your aim is to find enough people to audition; you should see at least five different performers for each major role. Places to look include local drama groups (consult your library, community centre, theatre, university), drama schools (particularly if they're nearby), personal contacts, and so on. If you want to find people from within the community, many local newspapers will print a story about you and your film, with contact details at the end. Or you can advertise: Some publications charge for this service, but others will provide it for free; be sure to include the relevant dates, the location, and the level of payment you're offering. Casting services exist on the Internet, and local organisations may also have websites and email addresses you can contact. There is also a publication called *Spotlight*, which lists all the actors in the country, with photos, and contact details for their agents. Unfortunately, it's very expensive in both paper and online forms, but they operate a telephone line which will supply you with the details of agents for any actor you care to name.

Unless you already know the actors, you should get hold of a photo and CV for each one, which will give you enough information to be able to whittle the numbers down to acceptable levels. Firstly, do they look right for the role? Bear in mind that the photos are not always entirely accurate. What's their experience like? If they've done loads of theatre but almost no film or television work, they are either unsuitable or very keen to gain experience. How old are they? As in any profession, those that do not succeed or have limited ability tend to give it up after a while. If you advertise for young actors, you will get vastly more applications than you would if you were looking for older actors; but the older actors are more likely to be competent.

Auditioning requires a room, a table, some chairs, and a video camera (make sure the actors say their name on camera to help you identify them later). One thing you must not do is audition anyone in your own home. One of the commonest horror stories is of the audition an actor went for at someone's flat which turned out to be run by just the one guy, whose requests seemed a little… inappropriate. So, get an audition room somewhere that isn't going to make the actors worry about their safety, and never audition alone - as much as anything else, the extra sets of eyes and ears will be invaluable.

How you audition people will vary according to what you want from them; if you want someone who can read the lines acceptably well, then that's all they'll need to do. If you want to see how they bounce off other actors, have them come in groups of one candidate for each character. Give them a chance to read for more than one character if possible. Bear in mind that, just as you're sizing them up, they'll be sizing you up. The more professional and accommodating you are, the more you will impress them; having somewhere to serve as a waiting room and giving them tea and coffee tend to help. I like to run my auditions as mini-workshops - get a group of actors together for maybe an hour, do read-throughs, and then experiment to see what they can add to the characters and story; most actors seem to find this approach refreshing after the cattle calls that most auditions resemble.

No decision should be immediate, but for a short film it should be possible to make your mind up and let the actors know within a week. Review your tapes. Discuss it with the people who were there with you. Check back over your notes. Choose the person you feel is right, but have a second choice as well; the first choice may turn out to be unavailable, especially if paid work turns up. Make sure they're happy to work for whatever you're offering, particularly if it's just expenses. Finally, once you have your cast confirmed, do everyone else the courtesy of a phone call to let them know.

Most agents I've had dealings with are very nice, helpful people. A lot of them will send out photos and CVs of their actors in reply to your ad despite the fact that there's no payment; but by and large, you're a very small blip on their radar. Many of your actors will be happy to deal with you directly; your dealings with agents will probably be minimal. But do be polite. So far as Equity goes, their influence over microbudget productions is limited. If your actors have agreed to work for expenses or a low wage, that's generally the end of it (unless you're at film school, in which case there are agreed rates you should already be aware of).

Crewing

On a feature film, you can expect to have a crew of at least fifty people working as a tight and efficient unit. On a short film, you may be able to get away with doing pretty much everything yourself - but you won't sleep much. Have a go at as many of the major jobs as possible just to get a feel for them and to make yourself aware of what's possible. The list that follows is not exhaustive, nor do you necessarily need everyone - at a minimum you need one person on camera and one person holding the microphone.

• **Producer** Responsible for organising pretty much everything with regards to the production and its subsequent distribution. Read the rest of the book.

• **Director** Responsible for interpreting the script into storyboards/ shotlists, the overall 'look' of the film, directing actors and crew during the shoot, working with the editor to get a cut of the film, directing the sound design.

• **Writer** Getting the script done. There's not much they can do on set, except as a consultant.

• **Assistant Director(s)** If you've got more than the most basic crew, you'll need an assistant director (AD). The AD's job is to keep the set running smoothly and ensure that the production stays on schedule. They take the hands-on organisational work off the shoulders of the director, leaving him or her free to concentrate on the creative side. The AD may also be responsible for directing crowds and extras. Runners report to the AD.

• **Director Of Photography/Lighting Cameraman** A Director of Photography (DoP) designs and implements the lighting for the film, supervises the camera operator, and plans the actual shots with the director. A Lighting Cameraman (or woman) is a DoP who operates the camera as well; you're better off finding one of these for your film, since it means one less crew member. Having a skilled DoP or Lighting Cameraman on your crew is an invaluable aid to an inexperienced director.

• **Camera Assistant** On larger shoots, assistants are required to take care of focus pulling, keeping the camera fed with batteries, cable bashing etc.

• **Gaffer** When there's a serious lighting kit to be dealt with, the DoP/ Lighting Cameraman is assisted by a crew of electricians ('Sparks'), of whom the leader is known as the 'Gaffer.' On a microbudget shoot, the Gaffer will probably be an assistant to the Lighting Cameraman. If you need a generator, you will have to hire a spark to operate it.

• **Sound Recordist/Boom Operator** The Sound Recordist is responsible for ensuring that dialogue is recorded as clearly as possible, and also collects any 'wildtracks' or 'atmos' required (see chapter on Sound for details). While it is possible to keep an eye on the levels meters and hold the microphone at the same time, it's better if you have one person monitoring the sound, and one person, a Boom Operator, keeping the microphone pointing in the right direction.

- **Grip** The Grip's responsibility covers any kind of mobile camera mounting, particularly 'dollies,' which are wheeled carts (running on tracks or tyres) on which the camera and operator sit while the Grip pushes them along. On a low-budget short the person not doing anything else tends to end up pushing the dolly.

- **Production Designer** On a professional production, the Production Designer is in charge of all aspects of design - sets, props, costume and so on - and runs the Art Department, with its legions of Wardrobe Assistants, Property Buyers, Carpenters and assorted useful people of all shapes and sizes. On a low-budget short, most of this will be done by you. It's not impossible to find a Production Designer to take this off your hands, but the need for a Production Designer implies complicated or large design requirements which are best avoided on your first few productions.

- **Continuity (Script Supervisor)** The Script Supervisor is responsible for making sure that you don't have continuity mistakes which disrupt the flow of the story, even when scenes that follow one another in the script are shot days or weeks apart. They keep a note of what each character was wearing in every scene, whether they used their left hand or right hand to perform an action, where objects were or how they were handled, and take Polaroids of performers and sets as a reference guide.

- **Make-Up Artist** The Make-up Artist is responsible for keeping everyone on screen looking as gorgeous or horrible as necessary. They usually need to be paid something to cover the use of materials, on top of other expenses. Most Make-up Artists can do minor prosthetic work (bullet holes and burns, for example), but anything larger will require a specialist.

- **Stills Photographer** One of the things that's often forgotten in the heat of the moment is that, for any film to sell, there must be stills to go with it. So get someone to take stills (with an SLR camera, preferably).

If you're just starting out, it's perfectly fine to use your friends to fill crew roles, especially when there's only a few of you. You might find yourself bargaining with a facilities house on the phone one minute, and pushing a dolly the next. You should make sure that someone in your group can drive - preferably over the age of 25 so they can drive a van.

It's very useful to have someone experienced around who can spot disasters before they happen and give you the advice you may desperately require. Make contact with your nearest media centre and ask if there's anyone who can help you out, or (even better) if you can volunteer for someone else's production, get some experience and end up with them owing you a favour. I highly recommend doing a stint as a lowly runner or assistant; it gives you an appreciation of the process which can rescue you when you make your own film.

Like actors, many crew are willing to work for nothing but expenses, but this only applies if they are in a similar position to yourself - looking to gain experience, develop their skills and build up a showreel. Lighting Camera people, Editors, Sound Recordists, Make-up Artists - anyone with a creative aspect to their work can be found. But some people are in this business to make a living and support a family; sparks, for example, are unlikely to give their time for free.

If you're recruiting, places to look include: the media centres already mentioned; film schools, which will have a number of students and recent graduates interested in gaining experience. Things like design and make-up will also be taught at local colleges, where students will be just as keen on getting some experience. *Shooting People* also allows you to advertise for crew; remember to specify what the wages and expenses situation is like, shoot dates and the part of the country you're shooting in. Crewing often works by means of personal contacts. You'll get more people if you've already made something yourself or have assisted on someone else's production.

Just as with actors, respect your crew as you would have others respect you. Expenses are a minimum if you're not simply drawing upon your friends and family, and a VHS copy for everyone is vital for people to be able to build up their showreels.

Props, Costumes & Make-Up

The first thing to do is to find out exactly what you need; break the script down into scenes and make a list of all the props, costumes and special make-up requirements mentioned in the script, and then a list of anything that might be required for set dressing. If you don't have things like costume actually specified in the script, make notes anyway on the sort of things you would like your characters to wear.

When making the list, make sure you note whether or not any of it will need to be dirtied, stained, damaged or destroyed in the course of the story. Say, for example, you have a shirt which must have coffee spilled down it; this is all very well for the first take, but unless that one went perfectly (very unlikely), you will need to go again, and you don't want to wait for the washing machine to finish first. What you do is get 'repeats' of the same item. Three should be a minimum - if you can't afford that, be very careful when you shoot.

As with everything else, the best props and costumes are the ones you don't have to pay for. If you have a contemporary story set in locations you already have access to, then you can probably get most the props and costumes with ease. But a 16th-century costume drama is going to need an enormous amount of work; don't attempt it unless you have the contacts to make it happen. The film industry is served by a number of specialist props and costume hire companies which are perfectly willing to negotiate a discount, but extremely unlikely to give away anything for free.

For contemporary stories, many actors will be willing to wear their own clothes. Ask them to bring a few possibilities for each individual change, and work together to see what's best. The high street should contain two places which will make your life easier - the charity shop and the pound shop. Charity shops are filled with all manner of clothes and other bits at ridiculously low prices. For any item of general clothing, they're worth a look; hang on to the receipt in case it doesn't fit. Pound shops are good places to pick up bits and pieces, not only for props but for many other things you might need when you're out on location; markets are similarly a good, cheap source. Costume hire shops abound, but generally they carry novelty stuff rather than authentic looking costumes; they're great for a gorilla suit, but not for a fully-realistic police uniform.

If you have a local theatre, it's worth making contact to see if you can borrow (or hire cheaply) anything from their props or costume stores. Getting to know your local theatre is good in more ways than one; there are often local companies and youth theatre groups attached, which can be good for finding actors with some degree of competence; they may have dedicated workshop space and construction staff who can advise you on possibilities for set construction or modification; and they may be willing to let you roam through their stores without let or hindrance. But do be considerate, and willing to offer your assistance to them in return.

Never underestimate the value of that which others throw away. Check around your contacts to see if there's something they want to offload either for free or a modest price. Do the same with organisations, if they have something you think you might need. Never be afraid to take a peek into a skip to see what potentially valuable item has been thrown away.

Using firearms or offensive weapons is a problem, as they can be dangerous to your cast and crew, and be mistaken for the real thing. Before using fake weapons of any kind, contact the police to warn them in advance - they're generally quite understanding and just as star-struck as everyone else. It is illegal to fire even blanks without a qualified Armourer on set, and these tend to be expensive.

For make-up, you really need a dedicated Make-Up Artist, but many things can be managed easily if you don't have one. A lot of people can handle their own make-up, and the main thing that's specifically required for filming is a little powder to reduce shine and soften the face (on men as well as women). You might even be able to manage more ambitious make-up work such as wounds and bullet holes. Morticians' Wax is available from most costume hire shops and can be moulded to create the shape of a wound. Blood can be bought (check to see if it's non-toxic if it has to go in the mouth), or you can make it with golden syrup and red food colouring (cochineal). Use a little coffee powder if you need to darken it.

Precautions

Emergency Services

Most of the time you won't need to inform the police of what you're doing, but bear in mind that if you are depicting any activity that seems illegal or dangerous, 'concerned' neighbours are all too capable of dialling 999 and getting the local armed response unit to scare you half to death. Calling the police and letting them know what you're up to is no more work than a phone call. Make sure you get the name and number of an officer you can contact if difficulties arise. It may also be worth leafleting the local residents to let them know what's going on, especially if you're likely to be shooting at night. If you're going to be setting fires, let the fire brigade know, but bear in mind that if they get a 999 call, they are obligated to attend even if they've been told about the fire beforehand. And most importantly, make yourself aware of the location of the nearest A&E unit, just in case you need to take someone there in a hurry.

Health & Safety

One of the key principles of our judicial system is that the accused is considered innocent until proven guilty. But not under health and safety law, and with good reason. The onus is on the defendant to prove that they took appropriate measures to ensure the health and safety of employees, participants and public; therefore, you are effectively guilty until you can prove yourself innocent.

Not that you have to stress yourself out if it's just you and a couple of friends messing around with a camera, of course, but as soon as you start getting more ambitious, take the time to work out all the possible things that can go wrong, and ways of making sure they don't.

Contracts & Legal

By and large, you will be unlikely to need to get anyone who works for you to sign a contract; the people you'll be working with should either be friends, people in the same position as you, or at least very understanding about the amount to which you'll be able to remunerate them. Even so, people have been known to become objectionable without warning, and it may be worthwhile to get people to sign a short agreement covering fees and rights. This does not constitute legal advice, which you should get before entering into any form of contract; this can be gained for free as part of the membership deals of some media centres and other organisations like the NPA (New Producers' Alliance).

Insurance

Public & Employer's Liability insurance protects you against claims by your cast, crew, or anyone else injured on your set, and is sold by specialist firms, but for many small films it's way too expensive to buy. However, professional cast and crew, and some locations, will expect you to be insured as a matter of course - your best bet is to work through your local media centre and see if they can cover you with their insurance. Equipment insurance is a separate matter - kit hired from media centres will already be covered, but professional hire companies will require you to get your own, or pay through the nose for their insurance.

Production

Organisation

In a perfect world, the day-to-day running of a shoot is handled not by the director but by the assistant director and his or her team of runners and assistants. In the real world (the one without any money in it), you might have an AD, but you will still be responsible for a lot of what follows. If you're just making a film with your friends on a more informal basis, you don't need to worry about everything - just do what seems sensible. Anything you forget will provide you with an unforgettable learning experience. If you're trying for a more advanced shoot, pretty much all of this will be relevant - something, somewhere on your shoot will go wrong, and having a belt and braces approach will help you cope.

Getting Everyone There

You need to make sure that everyone knows where and when to go. On professional shoots, call sheets are used to tell everyone what's going on in general, any special responsibilities they may have for that day, and how to get there. These need to be prepared every day to reflect the schedule changes which are likely on a long shoot; on a shoot lasting 3 to 5 days, however, you can get away with giving people a comprehensive schedule which includes their call times, along with maps and directions for how to get to the location.

Keep The Receipts

Get receipts for everything, preferably VAT receipts, which you need if you can claim VAT back. But even more importantly, make sure that the people whose expenses you are paying give you receipts for everything they've bought, as there's no other way of tallying up what you owe them (or being able to have a quiet word about spending too much of your money).

Backstage

The make-up artist is going to need somewhere to work, and they're going to need light. Actors will need somewhere to change, and preferably a place they can hang out when not on set. Tea and coffee will have to be positioned somewhere, usually wherever the kettle can be plugged in. Equipment needs to be piled up somewhere dry. Extras will have to have somewhere to wait. All of this has to be kept out of earshot or close enough so that people can hear you when you tell them to be quiet.

Shoot Ratios

The shoot ratio is the ratio of footage shot to the actual length of the film. A ten-minute film edited from 100 minutes of footage has a 10:1 ratio. Shoot ratios tend to be higher on video than on film, since the medium is cheaper and less technically tricky; a film shoot might be 6:1, but video shooting ratios may creep up to 20:1. Tape stock is one of the things that's difficult to get for free, so shooting less is a way of saving money - however, since many of the DV formats now have tapes of up to three hours in length, they work out quite cheaply and will give you the freedom to have a higher shoot ratio. However, putting all your footage on one tape is a significant risk - if you lose that tape, you lose your whole production, so there's something to be said for using lots of shorter tapes.

Closed Sets

On professional shoots, actors who are called upon to go partially or totally naked, or perform sex scenes, are protected by having a closed set - just them and a minimal crew, so they don't feel like they're being leered at by hairy crew members. This goes for male and female actors; it's nerve-racking enough taking your clothes off in front of a camera, and you don't need to make it any more difficult.

While it's unlikely that you'll be doing too much sex and nudity in your first few films - because a) it's difficult to persuade people to do that sort of thing, and b) do you really want to get that kind of reputation early on in your career? - you still may end up with scenes where people are down to their underwear or otherwise feel vulnerable. If in doubt, offer to make it a closed set and respect your actors.

The Routine For Doing A Take

Once the lighting's up and everyone's in place, run through the action for the benefit of the camera and boom operators, and study it closely on monitor and headphones to see if everything's working okay (you may want to discretely ask the camera operator to record this anyway - it might be good). Then it's time to go for a take...

• **Lock off the set** If you're in a public place, get runners to hold back pedestrians for the duration of the take.

• **Get some quiet** The AD yells at everyone to shut up. Absolute quiet is essential.

- **"Playback" (if necessary)** If you need music playing in the background (so people acting or dancing to it don't lose the rhythm), start it now. If dialogue is included in the scene as well, make sure you've practised the timing to have it switched off.
- **"Roll sound"** (If sound is being separately recorded and required for the take.)
- Sound Recordist reports "Sound rolling."
- Sound Recordist reports "Speed." (Tape recorders take a moment to reach full speed.)
- **"Turn over"** (Roll camera.)
- Camera Operator reports "Turning over."
- Camera Operator reports "Speed."
- **"Background Action"** If you have extras doing something specific (e.g. dancing), you may want them starting before the actors enter the scene.
- **"Action!"** After "Action!", actors may need separate cues to enter or perform an action. Practise this in advance.
- **"Cut!"** Wait for a few seconds after the scene is over to give yourself a little space in editing before you call cut. The camera operator can also call cut if things go wrong on their part. Actors can stop themselves if things go wrong. However, if they're deep into the scene and something beyond their control goes wrong, they'll usually find it irritating to have to stop.
- **Discretely ask camera operator if that was good** The people you need to talk to most after a take are the actors - but you also need to know if the take was technically okay. So have a brief word (or look) with the camera operator and sound recordist.
- **Check with the actors** Let them know what you thought of the performance and offer suggestions for the next take; as the takes go on, you may not have much to say, but at least give them some reassurance that things are going well. Be prepared to listen if they have ideas, but be decisive about your response to them.
- **Release any pedestrians you had waiting** Try and do this between takes if possible.
- **Repeat until you've got what you want** Doing only one take is unwise. You should shoot at least one more, known as a 'safety,' just to be certain you've got something. I find that a range of 2-5 takes is about normal.

Watching The Take

If you aren't the camera operator, and you have a monitor, you have a dilemma: do you watch the actors or the monitor? Watching the actors will give you a better idea of their performance - but tells you nothing about the framing and look of the shot. The monitor will tell you everything you need to know about the way things look - but may not give you the best view of their acting. Try both and see what you prefer. If you go for the monitor, try and keep it as close to the action as possible so that you can communicate with your actors and camera operator easily.

Protecting The Footage

The worst thing that can happen to your film is the footage going missing or getting damaged. Make sure there's a designated box the tapes go in while you're out on location, and never leave them lying around. You don't want to go through the experience of ripping a friend's van to pieces because you can't find yesterday's footage.

Reshoots & Pick-Ups

Once the shoot's over, it's not always over. In the industry, it's quite common to reshoot very large sections of a film after the initial edit and a sudden realisation that it just didn't work. Unfortunately, this costs money and is therefore unlikely to be an option for microbudget shorts. Negative Insurance could pay for reshoots in the event of losing the footage, but if you can afford that, you're not shooting on a microbudget. So you'd better damn well get it right... That said, some things can still be reshot after the shoot, particularly if they are small details like close-ups of a particular physical action or a prop doing something interesting. These are known as 'pick-ups', and you often find yourself doing just a few to correct eyelines or clarify actions or grab stuff that there just wasn't time to do in the first place.

Have A Nice Day...

Making films is supposed to be fun, for you and everyone else. Cast and crew will work better if they're enjoying themselves, especially when the hours are dragging on. Try and keep a good-humoured work environment for everyone, even if you're completely stressed out yourself. Allow for tea and coffee breaks. But don't let things get slack. Everyone collapsing in laughter at a fluffed line is fine once or twice, but the shot still has to be done. It's a delicate balance sometimes; helping out on someone else's film will give you a good sense of the right kind of atmosphere.

Shopping List

This is a not an exhaustive list; different situations will call for different bits and pieces, and you may not need everything on it - make your own judgements, but be prepared.

- **Car** All this kit needs to be moved somehow…
- **Shotlist, Storyboard, Script** Keep a couple of spare copies of each.
- **Money**
- **Map(s)** You never know when you may need to navigate through unfamiliar territory.
- **Gaffer Tape** Why is gaffer tape like the Force? Because it has a light side, a dark side, and it binds the universe together. An essential bit of kit for making sure that things don't fall apart, putting marks on the floor for actors, and so on. Also known as duct tape; hardware stores will stock it.
- **Camera Tape** (White electrician's tape.) If you're hiring bits of kit from different places, use this to label each piece so you know where it goes at the end of the shoot.
- **Lens Cloth & Brush** To keep the camera clean.
- **Stepladder** Handy for putting lights and props in high places.
- **Boxes** Large plastic ones available from pound shops and hardware shops. Not cardboard.
- **Safety Pins, String, Pen & Paper, Marker Pens**
- **Big Bits Of Card** To write complicated dialogue on if actors are having trouble with it.
- **Towels** If anyone's going in the water, or it looks like raining, towels are essential.
- **Toilet Roll** Because not all lavatories are civilised.
- **Cleaning Equipment/Products** Some locations have this stuff, but you should be prepared anyway.
- **Refuse Sacks** It's your responsibility to clean up after yourselves. Also very useful as waterproofing.
- **Kettle/Gas Stove (& Bottle)**
- **4-Way Mains Adapter** (At least two.)
- **Food & Drink** - Including: munchies (biscuits, chocolate etc.), tea & coffee (with decaf versions of both), hot chocolate, milk, sugar, cold drinks & water (if it's anywhere near summer).
- **Cool Box** For cold stuff.
- **Mobiles** Make sure these are turned off for shooting, but don't leave them behind.

- **First Aid Kit** It's useful to have someone trained in first aid as well.
- **Chairs** Director's Chairs are uncomfortable. Folding garden chairs are better.
- **Umbrellas** Large golfing types if possible. One with a pointy end which can be planted into the ground over the camera position is useful.
- **Wet Weather Gear**

Performers

Rehearsal

One of the most important things you can do is provide for rehearsal time in your schedule - about a day, shortly before the shoot (probably the day before) should be enough for most short films with a 3 to 5-day shoot. You'll need a room and a few chairs, plus maybe a table and as many props as you have available. Mark out the floor in the approximate shape of the location with gaffer tape or chalk, or, if you can arrange it, rehearse in the actual location.

You can use this time to go through the characters the actors are going to portray and invent background information that may be of assistance - it can be great fun brainstorming the backstory for a character, even if you have already worked out everything you thought you needed to know. A useful technique is 'hot-seating.' The actor sits in a chair and takes on the role of the character, and everyone asks them questions which they have to answer in character - use this to explore the type of person the character is, what they would do in certain situations, and to get the actor more involved with the character. Encourage actors to take notes about both their characters and the minutiae of performances, as details can easily be forgotten when shooting out of sequence.

The key is to cooperate with the actors, rather than give them orders. Actors thrive on interaction. You must be prepared to give them feedback on their work at the end of every run-through. Pay attention, take notes during the performance, and let them know what you think. "That's fine" or "I don't like that" aren't enough during rehearsal; explain in greater depth what you did or didn't like. Some directors believe that actors are nothing more than sophisticated tools (Hitchcock was blunter - he said they were cattle), and to some extent this is true - they are a component of a process which is larger than them, much more so than in theatre. But I find it more useful to think of them as collaborators - people who are there to help you create the story you set out to tell, and, hopefully, improve it.

The main reason to rehearse before filming is to save yourself time on set. You need to be responsive to your actors and to give them an input into building their characters - but rehearsing from scratch is a time-consuming business. You'll still need to do some rehearsing on set, but that's mainly for the benefit of the camera. You and your actors should be able to approach the shoot with a good idea of how you want to play the scene already lodged in your minds and notebooks.

When approaching a scene, it's worthwhile to get the actors to read it through once without prior preparation (a 'read-through'), just to see where they take it instinctively. This may not be the way you want to do the scene; subtext may be misinterpreted, lines delivered the wrong way, the scene may be too fast, too slow, too menacing, too fluffy, too static - but instead of jumping straight in to correct them, take the time to find out why it happened. The actors might have found a fundamental problem with the scene - for example, you may have a scene that is meant to be fast and pacy, but the dialogue takes too long to speak and needs to be cut.

Unless the actors have magically created the interpretation you wanted first time - and even if they have - spend some time breaking the scene down and going over it to work out what should be happening on a moment-to-moment basis - what the subtext is, what 'business' (physical actions) they can perform, whether or not the dialogue should be modified, whether anything can be added or subtracted to make the scene funnier, scarier, creepier, colder, warmer, joyful, depressing, or whatever else you think it should be. Let it be a collaborative process, but remember that, at the end of the day, you're in charge and you have the responsibility of steering the scene in the direction you want to go.

Many people find discussing and describing the nuances of performance difficult. You may feel the urge to demonstrate what you mean, rather than explain, but this is a bad move. It's a rather patronising way to explain something, and can be insulting. It also doesn't work as well; if an actor arrives at the correct performance under their own steam and with your guidance, they will know exactly why they're doing everything. But if you demonstrate something to them and try to skip over these stages, then they're just puppeting what you're doing, making for a phonier performance. Instead of demonstrating, think instead about rephrasing what you're trying to say, or working backwards to a point in the discussion before confusion arose, and deal with the underlying problems rather than trying to paste a demonstrated action onto the performance.

On Set

The first thing to do on set with the actors is to 'block out' the scene - deciding where people will be and what movements they will make around the set. Bear in mind where the camera's going to be and what sort of shots you're going to be using. If you were able to rehearse in the location, it will speed up this part of the process; in many sets and locations, however, this won't be possible, and you may have to adjust performances to suit the environment. Once the actors are fine with the scene, it must be rehearsed again for camera movements and any other technical requirements; this is not the time to make major changes to performance.

During shooting, you need to make sure that the actors are aware of what the shot size and framing are. In a long shot, actors need to be aware of their whole body and what it's doing, while facial expressions can be a little more exaggerated; in a close-up, they need to be careful not to overdo facial expressions, while at the same time, with the camera close in on them and them alone, they have the full responsibility of carrying the story and need to be at their best.

In dialogue scenes, you may not have all characters in shot at once. Technically, the people who are out of shot don't need to be there, but try and keep them around as it will assist the performer who's on camera. This is known as 'lines off.' However, don't bring an actor onto set if this is all you want them to do. When shooting phone calls between two locations, a member of crew can fill in the lines off for the performer who's supposed to be on the other end of the line.

Since sound cannot be recorded when there's loud background noise going on, actors will often find themselves having to pretend to shout over the sound of a crowd, or loud music, or airplanes taking off, or the end of the world or whatever. This is not a natural thing for people to do. So, if possible, turn on the music or get the crowd to talk for a while and have the actors practise the right level at which they have to pitch their voices. When actually shooting, keep an ear on them to make sure they keep up the right volume - it's very easy to slip, so just give them a gentle reminder if you need to. Something to watch for is complex movements that will have to be repeated in every take; is the actor reproducing the same movement each time? Are they getting the timing right? It's impossible to be perfect in every performance, but if they are doing wildly different things in each take - causing you major continuity problems - you'll need to take them aside for a moment and communicate this problem to them and find some way of overcoming it - possibly simplifying the action, or a moment of rehearsal to clarify it, or cutting it out altogether.

Extras

Extras don't need as much attention, and the job of directing them is often handed over to the AD. Their job is usually just to be there, but you (or the AD) do need to spend a moment to explain what's happening in the scene, and what they're required to do. You also need to make it clear that they must not look at the camera - the last thing you need to discover in the edit is an extra staring down the lens and then guiltily looking away.

Children & Animals

It's probably best not to. Children have limited attention spans and are rigorously protected by employment laws (although if it's your younger brother or sister on a small shoot during the holidays with very short hours, few are likely to complain). Animals are also protected by law, and cannot be forced to work; some animals may be able to do simple things if they think they're playing, but others will be difficult to persuade to do anything at all.

Camera

Before you go shooting, familiarise yourself with the camera. Most places you can hire a camera from should allow you to take a look at it before you take it away. Go through the manual page by page and make yourself aware of its abilities and if they're all working.

Things To Avoid

• **Automatic Functions** Most cameras come with little helpers like autofocus and auto-aperture - which only get in the way. You need as much control over your camera as possible, so locate anything automatic and switch it off.

• **Gain** A way to increase the brightness of a shot electronically. However, it makes the picture grainier and of lower quality.

• **Effects** Most of these are unnecessary because they apply an effect to the footage which you cannot get rid of later, and which therefore cuts down your options during the edit. Leave effects to later unless you have no other option.

• **Time Stamp** There's nothing worse than try to edit with a time stamp indelibly marked on the picture. Turn it off.

Lens

Not all lenses are the same; they vary according to how 'wide' or 'long' they are.

• **Wide angle lenses** pack more into the frame. In extreme cases, they distort the picture visibly, making things bulge out towards the viewer and look more 3D. They also have a large 'depth of field'; everything, or almost everything, will be in focus.

• **Long lenses** (also known as Telephoto lenses) are the opposite: they pack less into the frame and therefore things look much closer. They also look flatter, and a long lens will have a shallow depth of field; focus will have to be adjusted carefully to get a sharp picture.

• **Zoom lenses**, which you will get on most video cameras, are a combination of both: when zoomed out, the lens is wider, and when zoomed in, it is longer, packing less into the frame and making it look like you've moved closer to the subject. You will usually have a control marked 'W/T' (Wide angle/Telephoto) which allows you to zoom in and out. On cheaper cameras, you may only be able to do this at one speed; on better ones, you may be able to 'feather' it and have greater control.

Most video cameras will have a zoom lens, which is often not very wide even when it's zoomed all the way out. A few allow you to change lenses as you would on a film camera, or mount another on the front to modify the built-in lens.

Lenses should be cleaned with calotherm lens cloths, or the sort you use to wipe your glasses. Dust and marks on the lens are often invisible when shooting, but show up later when watching the film on a monitor.

Focus

Most cameras have a focus wheel on the lens which you can adjust manually. This is known as 'pulling focus' when you do it in the middle of a shot. In order to get perfect focus, you should zoom all the way into your subject, focus on them there, then zoom out. The subject now remains in focus at every stage of the zoom.

Aperture/Iris

The aperture, also known as the iris, is the gap through which light passes into the camera after being focused by the lens. It can usually be opened wider or closed down to allow more or less light through, depending on how much light there is in a scene. On video, you can usually judge it by eye with the viewfinder or a monitor.

Another effect of adjusting the iris is that the depth of field is affected. If the iris is closed down, then a lesser portion of the lens is being used to admit light, reducing overall picture quality, but increasing depth of field. Similarly, opening up the lens will decrease the depth of field.

Shutter

The shutter is the device which opens to allow light onto the receptors, and closes down between frames. The duration of time that the shutter is open affects the quality of movement on the screen. If the shutter speed is lower, it allows more time for objects to move - and so fast motions tend to blur. On high shutter speeds, the shutter opens for less time; movement no longer blurs, and objects stay solid. Some cameras will have a sports pre-set which will do this for you, but use a manual control if you have it. Beware of fluorescent lights, which tend to flicker when you film them at a high shutter speed.

White Balance

The human eye is more capable of adjusting to different lighting conditions than the camera. Light that you think is white may become pale blue or pale orange when the camera sees it. Mainly, the difference is between daylight and tungsten light (i.e. from normal light bulbs). The sun has a colour temperature of 5600°Kelvin while tungsten lights come in at 3200°K. Although daylight is 'hotter' in technical terms, the actual effect of blue light feels cold in comparison to the warm orangeness of tungsten light.

To adjust to this, you need to white balance the camera. Place a piece of white paper (or a white shirt, or white whatever) a few feet away from the camera, making sure it's lit by your light source. Zoom all the way in onto the piece of paper until it fills the frame, then press and hold the white balance button. The white balance symbol will flash in the viewfinder until the process is finished, and then turn solid. Pointing the camera at different coloured objects and white balancing to those can produce some interesting colour schemes. Experiment!

Normally, you will have to adjust white balance only at the beginning of a scene. Daylight and tungsten lighting are so different that you may have difficulties if both types of light are present in a scene. See the Lighting chapter for more information.

ND

Some cameras will have an ND ('Neutral Density') filter built into the lens mechanism; this is the equivalent of putting shades on the camera. Direct sunlight can be too much for a camera even when the iris is closed as far as it can go, so having an ND filter to cut down the light levels can be very handy on a sunny day.

Inputs & Outputs

• **Video Out** This will usually be of either the BNC, phono or S-Video type (your manual will tell you which you need and what they look like). It will usually be used to send video out to a monitor so you have a better picture to look at than the viewfinder can provide. If you want to output your video camera to your TV or video recorder at home, you will generally find you will have to plug the outgoing leads into a SCART adapter, which either comes with the camera or can be found in an electronics store.

• **Audio In** Not all cameras can accept incoming sound from an external microphone, but you should try and get one that does. The best audio leads are 'balanced' 3-pin XLRs (see Sound for details), though it may just be a stereo minijack on cheap cameras.

• **Audio Out** Again, XLRs are nice, but on most cameras these will be phonos and colour coded: LEFT AUDIO - Red, RIGHT AUDIO - White, VIDEO - Yellow. Some cameras will instead have an AV out socket, a minijack output which divides into the same three phono plugs

• **Headphones** This will usually be a minijack, but sometimes a full ¼" jack or phono. Make sure you get headphones to match the socket.

• **DV Out** DV cameras may well come with a 'DV Out' socket, which will send video and audio information through a 'Firewire' directly to a computer-based non-linear editing system. The benefit of this is that the signal does not have to be translated from digital to analogue, and will be preserved at highest quality.

Widescreen

There's a good reason for widescreen: take a look at your field of vision. You see the world in widescreen all the time. But widescreen isn't as simple as pressing a button and having a wider picture; for a start, you need to think about more than one widescreen ratio. Here are a few...

• **4:3 / 1.33:1 / Academy / Fullscreen** The basic TV shape, which is approximately the same as the 'Academy' screen ratio used in old cinema films. The basic frame of film is still this shape.

• **16:9 / 1.77:1** The widescreen ratio of new TVs, which many DV cameras will have an option for.

   • **1.85:1 / Extra-Wide** The basic ratio for most modern cinema films. This is accomplished by masking out the top and bottom of the screen. When shown on TV, many of these are shown in 'Pan and Scan,' zooming in on the picture and allowing the sides to be cut off, but panning from side to side if the subject is lost off the edge. Sometimes they are shown 'letter-boxed,' preserving the aspect ratio.

   • **2.35:1 / CinemaScope** Really serious widescreen, accomplished by optically squeezing the frame into an Academy shape with a special 'Anamorphic' lens. When projected, another lens unsqueezes the picture. When panned and scanned for TV, you can lose nearly half the screen with these films.

   The way 16:9 works for TV and video is by adapting the same trick used for CinemaScope: the 16:9 image is squeezed into a 4:3 frame when it's recorded, and when played back on a 16:9 TV or monitor, is unsqueezed again. However, this means that when you play the same footage back on a 4:3 TV, you will see the squeezed, anamorphic image - everything will look taller and thinner than it should. Unfortunately, not all editing systems are capable of unsqueezing 16:9 or changing into letter-box format for ordinary TVs; and also, the method used to get 16:9 on non-professional DV cameras isn't perfect and loses a little quality (though not very noticeably).

   If you want to bypass all of this, there's a much easier way of getting widescreen: gaffer tape. Put strips across the top and bottom of your monitor to simulate the shape you're going for, and frame accordingly (but don't try this directly into the lens). Most edit suites will allow you to put black bars at the top and bottom of the screen. Hey presto: instant widescreen.

Timecode

   Timecode is a counter which is recorded invisibly between frames, but which can be read by a VCR. It offers a way to identify and label every single frame separately - vital if you want to find anything when you're editing. Simply having a counter on the camera does not guarantee timecode - it may just be a counter. Check your manual to make certain. Timecode appears in the format HH:MM:SS:FF, e.g. 10:34:22:24, and can be pre-set to begin at any point you wish. Hour numbers on each tape you shoot should be different, so it's easy to tell the tapes apart (this doesn't work if the tapes are longer than an hour). You should try and leave the camera in pause record between takes, as rewinding back to check previous takes, or taking the tape out, can result in discontinuous timecode, which will confuse your editing system later on. Also, record a good 30 seconds of nonsense at the beginning of each tape to allow for Preroll (see Editing).

Power & Batteries

If your camera is nowhere near a wall socket, you'll need batteries. Always carry more than you think you'll need; you'll almost certainly end up using them. Batteries for video cameras are all rechargeable, but older nickel-cadmium batteries suffer from what is called the 'memory effect'; they must be fully discharged before being recharged, or they will not fully recharge. They seem to 'remember' the point at which they stopped being used, and only recharge that far. Modern lithium batteries suffer from no such problems, and can be recharged fully from any state of discharge. You should make yourself aware of how long the batteries last, and how long they take to recharge; get them charged up before you go.

Analogue Tape Formats

• **VHS/S-VHS/VHS-C** (No Timecode) Great for practising on and making viewing copies, but not much else. S-VHS is an enhanced version, and VHS-C is a pint-sized version. Digital VHS was waiting in the wings at time of writing.

• **8mm/Hi-8** (No Timecode) Before Mini-DV this was the format of choice for the guerrilla video maker. Small and handy, but now on the way out.

• **U-Matic/U-Matic SP** (Timecode) University and College film studies departments all over the country have the remnants of this obsolete near-broadcast quality format lurking around.

• **Betacam SP** (Timecode) The basic broadcast format. If you need to deliver your film to a festival or TV company, this is a format that everyone will accept.

Digital Tape Formats

• **Mini-DV** (No Timecode) Now the basic consumer format. The sound and picture quality you get vary enormously, depending on the camera. Most consumer ones are a damn sight better than VHS.

• **DVCAM** (Timecode) Near as dammit broadcast quality. If you want your film to look like you shelled out some serious money, choose this.

• **DVCPro/DVCPro 50** (Timecode) The original DVCPro was under-developed, and rectified in the DVCPro 50 version, but doesn't have much of market outside ENG (Electronic News Gathering).

• **Digital S** (Timecode) Digital S is an excellent format - comparable to Digibeta - but very hard to find.

• **Betacam SX** (Timecode) A professional format; Beta SX is a sort of half-breed with an odd attitude to compression. It's cheaper than Digital

Betacam, but used a lot less.

• **Digital Betacam** (Timecode) Digital Betacam (or 'Digibeta') is more or less the top dog at the moment, especially for drama. On the other hand, it costs the earth. Many festivals and TV stations accept Digibeta as a delivery format, and there's not much that's better for making a final master of your film.

Monitors

Virtually all cameras have a video out socket which allows you to plug in a monitor. These are quite tiny, up to about 6" across, and the settings on the monitor - brightness, contrast, colour etc. - often affect the picture enough that you can't be exactly sure what the picture quality is like (unless your camera can output colour bars, which will allow you to calibrate the monitor to the camera); but at least you can check framing and know what's visible and what's not. If you're getting your equipment at a media centre, they should have a monitor they can hire you as well.

Some cameras have another nice toy - an LCD screen which flips out from the side, and can be reversed so that you can shoot yourself and see yourself at the same time. This is great for 'video diary' shots, but beware - LCD screens of that size are even worse than normal monitors for showing true contrast, brightness or colour, and can easily become almost invisible in direct sunlight. They're best as a framing guide.

180° Rule

Also known as 'crossing the line.' This is one of the most fundamental, and yet easy to break rules of camerawork. Simply put, if you're filming two people, you need to keep the camera on one particular side of them, because if you cut to a shot on the other side, the mind is unsettled.

Imagine you have two characters: Mr West and Ms East. Draw an imaginary line between them, running West to East. Say the camera is south of that line; it can cut between shots favouring either Ms East or Mr West, over-the-shoulder shots even (Cameras 1 & 2 on the diagram), but what you cannot then do is cut to a camera position which is in the north (Camera 3). That's crossing the line. Partly, it's a problem of the viewer suddenly seeing what seems like a reversal of the positions of the two characters (you can even end up making two people who are looking at each other seem as if they are both staring off in the same direction), and partly it's a problem of the sudden change of background to something previously not established. The problem can easily be solved if you have a shot during which the camera moves from south to north; but once you're in the north, you've still got that line between the characters, and cutting to a camera position in the south would be crossing the line again.

The problem becomes more complicated as you put more characters into a scene. Even experienced directors and camera operators can screw up when it gets complicated. It's possible to use the unsettling effect of crossing the line deliberately, but make sure you first know how to avoid the problem.

Crossing The Line Example:

NORTH

CAMERA3 X

MR
WEST

MS
EAST

THE LINE

CAMERA1 ✓

SOUTH

CAMERA2 ✓

Eyelines

One of the trickiest things to do when filming actors is to get their eyelines right. From the simple question of "do they look to the left or the right of the camera?" to subtle graduations to make it look like they're eyeballing different objects or people within a single shot, you need to be aware of what shots are going to be next to each other in the edit, and where people will be looking in all those different shots. Making a mistake with an eyeline can make an actor look like they're addressing the window when they're supposed to be staring daggers at someone in the middle of the room.

Framing For Storytelling

The way in which you frame a character on the screen can have an enormous effect on the way the audience sees that character. Here are a few examples:

- **Relationships** If two characters are put together in a frame, it draws them together; if they are kept in separate frames, even if they are physically close, it seems to put some space between them. You can say a lot about a marriage in this way. In *Casablanca*, Rick and Ilsa are almost always shown in the same frame together, but Ilsa and Victor Laszlo - the man she is married to - are often separated, not just by separate framings but by placing objects between them on the screen; a lamp or a pillar, for example. It helps us understand instinctively that they aren't much in love.

- **Power** A character who is high in a frame will usually seem more powerful than a character who is lower (you should bear this in mind when casting as well as framing). Orphaning someone on the left or right of the frame if they're talking to someone who is centrally framed in another shot says plenty about their power relationship. Distance from the character also has an effect; if someone is smaller in frame, they will usually seem less powerful, especially when compared to someone who's much larger in frame.

- **Looks & Implications** The amount of space you leave above, below, or to the side of a character or object can say a lot about what else is going on outside the frame. We've all seen the shot where a vast amount of space was left beside a character, making us think something's about to come in from that direction. More simply, if characters are looking in a certain direction, you can place them to either the left or the right of the frame to suggest the space they're looking into. This is a common technique when two people are looking at or talking to each other. And anyway, always having the subject in the centre of the frame is boring.

- **Headroom** Beginners instinctively put the face central in the frame. Unless the face is already filling the frame, this can leave a rather large and empty looking space above the character. Instead, you need to put the head higher in the frame and leave a strip of 'headroom' above them.

- **High And Low Angles** If the subject is shot from below, they seem more powerful and dynamic, and if they are shot from above, they seem weaker and less capable of changing their world. But bear in mind that most people don't look good from a low angle.

Framing For Widescreen

Widescreen is great for landscapes, which is why westerns and road movies often use it. However, faces are more vertical than horizontal; a 4:3 frame allows you to go close on a character and have them fill the frame, but in widescreen formats the same size shot will leave space at the side - the framing effects can be very nice, but not everyone likes it.

Another thing that widescreen can do is pack more characters into a frame. If you're doing scenes where characters are sitting or standing beside each other, you can accommodate more of them at the same shot size than you could with 4:3.

Camera Movement

Moving the camera, like cutting to another shot, should only be done when there is motivation for the move. Having the camera move for no apparent reason, or not as part of an overall style, is distracting. Here are some things to bear in mind:

• Tracking vs. zooming. I usually prefer tracks, because they feel like a more natural movement - perspective changes and you actually feel like you're moving. Zooming looks more mechanical when done in place of a track. Zooms are often useful as a very slow movement into or out of a frame; the change can be barely visible, but still gives a powerful effect.

• Tracking/zooming toward a subject has the effect of drawing the audience closer. Look at me! it shouts, partly because we're all programmed to pay attention to objects approaching us (especially if moving at speed), and partly because there's less to look at in the frame. Tracking out tends to make a character look lonely and less powerful, isolated and vulnerable. It's also a good way to close a scene or the film itself; the extra visual information entering the frame makes it look very profound. Just remember that you have to light all the extra information.

• In the industry, tracking is literally done on tracks. These are laid out by the grip, who then pushes a 'dolly' (a mobile camera mounting) back and forth on them. This can be expensive, but simulating it is surprisingly easy; firstly, you need something to act as a dolly - a wheelchair, pushchair or pram are all good (gaffer taping a camera tripod to a pram chassis is a great trick). These are fine by themselves over smooth floorings; on other surfaces, cardboard or plywood sheeting can be useful to make a smooth 'track.' Hand-holding the camera while sitting in a wheelchair is another good one.

• It's possible to track back from a subject while simultaneously zooming into it (or the other way round). While the subject will appear to remain static, everything around it will change according to the changing properties of the lens - seeming to be stretched or compressed in a very eye-catching way. Famous uses of this: done fast in *Jaws* (Roy Scheider sees the shark) and done slowly in *Goodfellas* (Ray Liotta, sitting in a diner, realises he is about to be executed by the mob).

• Pans and tilts are accomplished with a tripod. A good tripod should be an invaluable tool on any shoot, but don't use stills tripods as a substitute - they're not designed to take the weight of most video cameras.

• An otherwise unmotivated pan or tilt can be used as a way of getting into or out of a scene.

• Hand-holding the camera allows you to do whatever you like, but it has an additional effect: because it's not a straight-line geometric move-ment, and because it's naturally a bit shaky, the overall field of vision is wider, and more akin to the way your eyes work; so it makes the subject feel more natural.

Cheating

Actors and props don't always have to be left in exactly the same place when you move the camera for a new angle. Very often, it will be impracti-cal or time-consuming to do so. For example, the wall behind a character may not be properly dressed, but you still need to do the shot right now. 'Cheating' them round a little to edge out the offending section of wall will not offend the eye when you cut the sequence together. The only consider-ation is: "will it cut together in the edit?" If it will and you can save time and effort by cheating, do so.

Lenses

Your choice of lens (or your choice of how far to zoom in) affects the visual quality of the picture. Wider lenses allow for a frame with more visual information packed in, and have a larger depth of field; this makes them a more naturalistic way of presenting things. More extreme wide lenses have the effect of creating disturbing images as the subject seems to bulge out towards us as it grows closer. Longer lenses flatten out the picture and make the depth of field shallower, making the image more beautiful, due in part to the out-of-focus areas of the screen. You can pull focus during a shot to suddenly or slowly change the part of the screen or the subject that the viewer is looking at.

If you're using more than just the standard zoom lens on your camera, watch out for 'vignetting,' where the edge of the lens becomes visible in the frame. This, unsurprisingly, is something you want to avoid.

Filming Computer Screens

Computer monitors do not run at the same frame rate as TV and Video (25 fps), and will therefore appear to flicker when filmed. A 'phase converter' will adjust the frame rate of the computer, but will cost you money. My advice is to film any computer screens as cutaways and use the screen of a laptop instead of a monitor; laptops use continuously glowing LCD displays rather than cathode ray tubes, creating a slight after-image effect, but eliminating any flicker.

Camera Insulation

If you're in a very quiet environment, you may be able to make out the whirring motors of the camera and find that sound is having a problem. In this case, it's time to get someone to sacrifice their jumper or jacket and use it to 'blimp' the camera. In the event of rain, you'll find that, even if you have an umbrella over the camera, it will be wise to wrap it in a refuse sack anyway. Rain can easily dribble in despite the umbrella holder's best intentions.

Condensation & Dust

When moving from a cold to a warm environment (e.g. from a cold exterior to a heated swimming pool), water may condense on the inside of the camera. Some cameras will flash up a warning light when this happens; if it's not there or you don't pay it heed, the camera will at best be clogged up by the tape getting wet, and at worst be an electrical hazard. To avoid this, acclimatise the camera slowly; wrap it up in a black sack or put it in its case, and allow it to sit for fifteen minutes and reach the ambient temperature. Take the tape out so that it can acclimatise separately. Cameras are also vulnerable to dust or sand that gets inside the casing; if this is likely to happen, wrap the camera up well and keep a brush handy to clean the damn stuff off.

Lighting

The basic purpose of lighting is to make sure that your camera can see the subject. But lighting can also be invaluable to give information about character, setting and mood. It isn't the first thing that most people consciously notice, nor should they. But it does influence the way they see the film - quite literally.

Most lighting is about creating the illusion of reality; poorly lit images can look very flat and unnatural. Putting the right combination of light and shade onto an object gives it depth. A subject lit in this way is said to have greater 'modelling.' We need to see shadows as well as light in order to get a feeling of the shape of a face. You usually need to see the actors' eyes as well, so be careful about putting people in shadows.

Hard Light/Soft Light

Hard light is directional, and throws a distinct shadow; soft light bounces around in all sorts of directions, and throws an indistinct shadow (if any). Soft light is less powerful when coming from the same source as hard light, because so much of it is heading off into other directions - half the intensity or more can be lost.

Most naked lights (e.g. clear glass tungsten bulbs and the sun) produce comparatively hard light; soft light can be made from this in a number of ways. The most simple is to bounce it off a light coloured surface, scattering it. Using walls, floors and ceilings is possible, but you can also make, buy or scrounge various kinds of reflectors (see below). Another way is to 'diffuse' the light. A kind of paper called 'trace' can be pegged in front of the light, or put across a window through which hard light is shining. Normal paper is no good for this, because it will start to burn. Photographic shops and media centres should have supplies. Smoke machines are also good - pumping lots of smoke into the air and wafting it about until it is finely distributed will diffuse all the light in the scene (but make sure the smoke detectors are off). And you can stretch a stocking over the lens, diffusing the light coming into the camera. This sort of thing only tends to get used for close-ups on an individual subject, because it's indiscriminate about what it diffuses. Also, you can simply move the light closer - if you do this, more of the light which is heading off at wider angles will fall on the subject, making the overall light more scattered and softening shadows (and if you want to make shadows harder, move the light further away).

A combination of soft and hard light is usual in most scenes. Faces are flattered by soft light, but may need a little hard light to add definition. Hard light is good for backgrounds, especially when you're on a longer lens, putting them a little out of focus.

Three-Point Lighting

The most basic and simple lighting set-up. The three points are three light sources:

• **Key Light** A bright, hard light usually positioned in front and slightly to the side of the subject. Provides the main illumination, but throws some nasty hard shadows. Makes features seem a little flat.

• **Fill Light** Also in front of the subject, and towards the other side, should be a diffused light source throwing a softer light onto the subject. This eliminates as much shadow as possible (as a softer light, it won't be throwing much shadow itself) and to flatter the subject a little. But this still leaves things a little flat. So..

• **Back Light** A light source from somewhere behind and above the subject is used to add a little light to the rear of the subject, and distinguish from the background. This rounds out the subject and gives it a bit of modelling

While this is mostly used only for interviews, it's still a good starting point. The basic ideas of key light, fill light and back light form the bedrock of more complex set-ups. Key lights are often diffused to make people look prettier. Bear in mind that fill light and back light can just as easily come from reflectors as from anything else, and those reflectors can be positioned anywhere (however, being lit from beneath is not very flattering to most people, unless they need to look like a serial killer). Another interesting thing is that the lighting style of film noir - harsh black and white edges, shadows being thrown everywhere, high contrast between light and shade - can be easily produced just by getting rid of the fill light.

Available Light

You can save yourself a lot of time, money and stress by using the sun as a light source. The sun works well as a key light, and you can use reflectors to bounce back the same light, effectively creating other sources.

The sun can be a bit overpowering, especially when it's forward of the camera (contrast between the sky and subject can be so much that either the sky will be solid white, or the subject will be too dark to see). There are two ways to cut down available light - you can use a Neutral Density filter on the camera, or (if you're inside) a sheet of the same stuff (media centres and photographic shops should stock it) on the window. Or, if you want to be a bit more selective, you can use black drapes (or any large, flat non-reflective surface - polyboard can have one side painted black) to create "negative bounce" and remove some of the reflected light.

Shooting towards the window through which the sun is coming is tantamount to filming into one of your lights, and you get the same effect: it burns out on the screen. You will have to work hard to decrease the contrast between the amount of light in the window and the amount of light in the room; again, ND on the window or more light within the room will help.

The sun has a tendency to move, and you will have to compensate. Shoot wide first to get the master, which will show the largest amount of area the sun is shining on. Then do your closer shots, in which you can exercise more control over the lighting with reflectors and adjust to the changing position of the sun while concealing the change.

A neat trick when outside is to use the sun as a back light while shooting towards it; with reflectors to provide key or fill lights; the directly reflected light will be perfectly fine.

High Key/Low Key

Two classic styles of lighting are known as High Key and Low Key (neither of which have anything to do with the term 'key light'). This is as much a question of production design as anything, but here are the basics:

• **High Key** Generally more light in the frame. Less contrast overall. Everyone seen very clearly, and shadows largely kept to a minimum. Light tends to be softer.

• **Low Key** Less light overall, but what light there is provides a much higher level of contrast within the frame. Shadows could well be all over the frame, and anything could be in them. Faces may not be completely lit. Light often harder.

For an example, contrast the look and style of *Ally McBeal* and *The X-Files*. One is a light-hearted show blowing up the trivia of relationships into comedy drama; one is a paranoid conspiracy/crime/supernatural thriller. No prizes for guessing which is high key and low key. Note that these styles are not rigorously pursued through every scene of either series; in *Ally McBeal*, the bar scenes are often low key, and the *X-Files* has less low-key lighting in daytime exteriors, particularly when the exterior happens to be a snow field (a natural reflector).

Colour Temperature

The hotter a light source is, the bluer the light it will give out; the colder, the more orange. Light sources are conveniently split into two groups - tungsten (orange), so called because this is the element used to make the filaments of light bulbs, and daylight (blue), which includes the sun but also 'daylight-balanced' lights.

The camera can adjust to either of these with the white balance control (see Camera), but when both types are present, you have to take some action to sort it out. This is done with gels; rolls of translucent plastic sheeting which come in a variety of colours for cosmetic and effects purposes, but can also change the colour temperature of the light coming through them. A blue gel turns tungsten light into daylight, an orange one turns daylight into tungsten.

Gels can be clipped (with wooden or metal pegs, not plastic ones) onto the barn doors of a light in order to change them; if you have the sun outside, you can put orange gel over the window to turn it tungsten and match your interior lighting.

Not every environment in the real world is naturally so balanced. There are little discrepancies everywhere - in a single room, direct sunlight may come from one window, and reflected sunlight from another, which has a slightly lower colour temperature. Man-made lighting has created such mixes all over the place. You may approach a ticket office in a train station with the sun to one side and tungsten (or fluorescent, or both) coming from the inside of the booth. Sometimes things are a little mixed, though you will usually have to mute the contrast between the different colour sources to allow the camera to cope.

Fluorescent Lights

Fluorescent lights are neither tungsten nor daylight; instead of coming out blue or orange, they have a greenish light. The white balance control can adjust to this, but the same problem of mixture with other light sources remains. Gels are available to modify lights to match fluorescent light - 'plus green' to modify daylight and tungsten, and 'minus green' (actually pink) to modify fluorescent to tungsten. But mainly, the best thing to do is not to mix fluorescent with anything - either use just fluorescent and colour balance to it, or switch them off and use other lights.

Types Of Lights

Lights are measured by their wattage; light bulbs at home are either 40, 60 or 100W, while a standard fluorescent tube is about 70W. Film lights can go up to 18,000W (18kW) or more - useful if the sun won't come out and play.

Domestic lights are usable if you have nothing else. They can be augmented by getting a few 500 watt photoflood bulbs from a photographic shop. Your light fittings and lamps at home will not be designed to cope with this much power, so you'll need to get a special one with brass fittings.

Theatre lights are not too useful, since they are designed for the eye rather than the camera. Film lights can be hired from media centres, or from a university or college that teaches the subject. Professional hire companies are more expensive and require you to pay for your own insurance, whereas the others will already have this dealt with.

The basic film lights are known as Redheads (800W) and Blondes (2,000W/2kW), which gives you some idea of what sort of people were working in the industry in the early days. Redheads come in packs of three and are standard interview equipment; Blondes are a higher-powered accompaniment. Neither of them have fresnel lenses, but they're excellent lights to work with when you're learning the basics. Lights with fresnels come in various wattages and have many names - if they're available, get them.

Very small lights (100W or thereabouts, sometimes called 'birdies') are good if you need to put in a little highlight to make things more interesting; 12V battery lights are handy for this kind of work, especially at night, and are also good for wrapping when it's pitch black outside and you've just turned all the other lights off to cool down.

Daylight balanced lights of the HMI or MSR type are available from professional suppliers. They both have fresnel lenses, but HMIs are older, bulkier and heavier, and flicker; it's best to get the 'flicker-free' variety which are more expensive but less of a headache. MSRs are more expensive still but a lot less hassle. You'll need a dedicated stand to hold each one, since they're all quite heavy. Each comes with a 'ballast,' a transformer which amplifies the power from the ring main and must itself be turned on before the light can operate. While these lights may be very expensive, they do give out twice as much light as tungsten lights for the same wattage - it's worth getting hold of a 1.2 kW HMI or MSR on more advanced shoots, if you can manage it. This is the maximum size you can run off a domestic ring main, and it makes an excellent key light for most situations. On nighttime exteriors it can be invaluable, and when placed outside a window, can turn a night interior into a day interior. If you use one of these lights, make sure you get them fully demonstrated to you - they require a little more care and attention than smaller lights.

Fresnels/Spotting/Flooding

Most lights intended for film or photographic use have a control on them which allows you to 'spot' or 'flood' the light. This will make the light more directional (spot) or make it spread out more (flood); it also changes the area the light shines on, and the intensity. Another thing that will make a light more directional is a 'fresnel' lens on the front of the light. This is a scaled-down version of the lenses used to make spotlights almost completely directional, and assists greatly in making the light controllable. Lights without a fresnel are basically naked light bulbs with only a reflector at the back, and will therefore be more prone to scattering light everywhere.

Increasing/Decreasing Light On A Subject

If you decide that you need to make things brighter or darker, there are five basic options:

• Walk the light in or out, ensuring that it's switched off first. Bear in mind that the amount of light hitting a subject will decrease exponentially the further away the light is - taking it out to twice the distance will mean that a quarter of the light falls on the subject, rather than the half that you might have expected.

• Spot or flood the light. This is a pretty fine adjustment but it may be all you need.

• Open or close the aperture on the camera. Not advised due to the effect on picture quality and depth of field - it'll be a major job to adjust everything.

• Removing/replacing diffuser. Although this will have an enormous effect on the amount of light hitting a subject, it will quite possibly screw up the overall lighting set-up.

• Turn the light slightly and thus move the subject closer or further from the brightest part of the light's output, the centre. This can cause problems elsewhere in the lighting set-up which will need to be rectified.

Shooting At Night

There are two types of night for lighting purposes: 'real' night, without any light source (other than stars and moon, which are too dim to be of practical use); and the sort of night-time you get in cities, where artificial lights of all kinds abound. To make shooting 'real' night a possibility, take the biggest light you have and place it very high up behind the subject (out of a window or on a big stand), make sure it's got blue gel over it and then colour balance your camera for tungsten light. Everything becomes rather blue and monochrome - which is what your eyes see under moonlight.

Recreating artificial light is fairly easy; if it's already there in the environment (like street lights) you can use reflectors just as though it were available light. Otherwise, use your lights to mimic whatever would normally be there. Some cameras will come with lights mounted on top; these are intended for documentary use and not much good if you want naturalistic light.

Out in the wilderness there are unlikely to be sources of power. In the industry, generators ('gennies') are used; but the smaller versions you might consider for use on a microbudget production are often very unreliable. Some hardware hire shops carry them, but these are not intended for film use; you'll have to check the power output and match it to the requirements of your lights carefully. You'll also need someone to look after the genny and keep it safe - the job of a spark. So generally, it's not recommended.

Safety

Sticking a bunch of extremely hot lamps with large amounts of electricity running through them up onto high stands which are sometimes more wobbly than we'd like creates a number of health and safety issues...

• **Heat** Lights are too hot to touch. When turned off, they need time to cool down. Some smoke detectors will set off a fire alarm if a hot light is placed beneath them. You may notice some smoke coming off a light when you turn it on; this is probably dust burning off, and nothing to worry about.

• **Light** When turning lights on, shout "eyes!" as a warning. Lights should, wherever possible, be used above or below eye level, since they can dazzle or damage the eyes of performers. Children are easily distracted by bright, hard lights; softening the lights you use on them will help to avoid both dazzle and loss of concentration.

• **Power** Domestic ring mains are only capable of bearing so much - 13 amps per power point (not per socket!). To find out the amperage of a light, divide the wattage of the light by the voltage of the power supply (240V in the UK, 110V in the US). Redheads: 800W/240V = 3 amps. Blondes: 2000W/240V = 8 amps.

• **Water** Electricity and water do not mix, although HMI/MSR daylight balanced lights can get hot enough to make drizzle evaporate the moment it hits them. But in worse conditions they must be protected, the same as other lights. Cables should be kept dry in all circumstances, especially where they join to other cables. Some of the plastic boxes you might be using to carry props or goodies are useful as a basic 'umbrella,' while wrapping them in bin bags or cling film are other methods.

• **Topple** If lights are up high on stands, weight the stands at the base with sandbags or stage weights, or anything else that is particularly heavy. And you must never put a light onto a stand for which it is not intended.

Reflectors

Reflectors are a basic but handy tool for the microbudget cinematographer, and can easily be scrounged or made. The professional kind are called 'lastolites' and are a circular frame inside which is stretched reflective fabric; this frame twists and folds into a smaller shape for storage. They usually have a white side and a silvery side; the latter reflects light more directionally and provides harder light.

Polyboards (great big sheets of polystyrene) are available in the industry as 8' by 4' sheets, and usually painted black on one side for negative bounce. They're not terribly expensive and the same material is often used as insulation in building. It's possible to scrounge or buy from builders' yards. It can be cut down to smaller sizes for more finicky work - a 4' by 4' shape is common.

You can make a reflector quite easily. You need a white sheet, something flat (or a frame of some sort), and wooden pegs to clip the sheet on. If you need harder light, clip kitchen foil on instead. Better still, use both - one on each side.

Black drapes are something that theatres and other public venues are most likely to have; borrowing them is a matter of making friends with your local theatre people. Of course, the material can be bought, but will tend to be expensive.

More Ways To Control Light

Most lights come with barn doors on the front: four doors which open outwards to let light out. They can also be used to control light, and closed down to get rid of flare, or turn the light into a thin bar of illumination - handy for little cosmetic touches. When barn doors aren't enough, you can use 'flags,' which are any large, flat object light enough to be easily moved around. If the light from one lamp is going into the wrong place, you can put an edge on it by 'flagging it off.'

Light on its own can sometimes be boring. One way to make things more interesting is to interpose a 'gobo' between the light and the subject. A gobo is anything that breaks light up and puts a natural-looking pattern onto the subject. A favourite is a small tree branch gaffered or clamped to a lighting stand.

Flare

Lenses sometimes catch the light in such a way that it produces 'lens flare,' which is not always pretty. It often shows up as a small patch of light on the screen, where it only gets in the way. The light that causes the problem must be 'flagged off.' Place a flag between the light that's causing the problem and the camera, and carefully adjust to make sure that the flare is removed but no interference with the lighting set-up has been made. You can also use the barn doors to do the same thing, but this is more likely to have an effect on the lighting set-up.

Stands & Clamps

Most lights come with lighting stands - basically, tripods with poles on them. It's a good idea to have a few stands spare, as these can be used to hold flags, polyboards, gobos and other assorted odds and ends aloft. You can also get a kind of stand called a 'polecat,' an extendible pole with rubber 'feet' on each end which can be wedged between floor and ceiling. Clamps are then used to hang lights from it.

The basic 'Italian clamp' consists of a grip which can be applied to any surface (or slid onto a stand), and a mounting for lights. Another kind is known as a 'magic arm' and is jointed to allow enormous flexibility of positioning. They're mostly useful for lighter bits and pieces; small lights, flags etc.

Sound

When shooting film, sound is recorded separately from the picture, usually on either DAT (Digital Audio Tape) or ¼" reel-to-reel tape, though some lower-budget productions use MiniDiscs. Therefore sound and picture will have to be synchronised in post-production; every shot is marked with a clapperboard (known as a "slate") which visibly makes a sharp sound to allow picture and audio to be matched. On video, sound is recorded directly onto the same tape, and automatically synched. A slate is only required if you need to have a visual marker for each shot, or are using two cameras and want to record the sound onto just one of them. But otherwise, recording sound for video requires exactly the same care and attention as it does in film, and should be the job of at least one person throughout the shoot.

Digital/Analogue

If sound is recorded analogue, it will be laid down as a waveform; if it's being recorded digitally, then the sound will be digitally sampled thousands of times each second. The practical difference is that analogue sound needs to have input levels set very carefully - if it's too quiet, the sound will be lost in hiss and be useless. Digital formats effectively have no hiss (unless they're copying from an analogue format, in which case the hiss will be reproduced perfectly). They usually have a control which allows you to select a sample rate; the possibilities are 36 kHz, 44.1 kHz (CD sample rate) or 48kHz. The higher the sample rate, the more information is encoded, and the more space that information takes up; therefore the tape will run faster, and won't last as long. While it's best to record at the highest quality possible, it's difficult to tell the difference.

Cables & Inputs

Sound can be carried on two types of cables - 'balanced' or 'unbalanced.' Unbalanced leads (like phonos or minijacks) carry the signal upon a single wire. But over more than a few feet they pick up radio signals (usually Radio 4, for some reason). Balanced leads, called XLRs (or cannons), have three wires in each cable and through some clever trickery make radio interference cancel itself out. Most consumer cameras will have no sound inputs at all, apart from sometimes a single unbalanced minijack. Higher-end consumer cameras and all professional cameras will have two XLR inputs. Many microphones will only plug into an XLR. Outputs also vary; on most professional equipment, it is assumed that the camera will not be used for playback, and outputs do not exist. On consumer equipment, there are usually two phonos.

Headphones

Incoming sound should be monitored at all times, and all cameras have a headphone socket. This is often a minijack, but on some models may be the larger ¼" jack. Make sure you get the appropriate set of headphones, although a pair of earplugs from a Walkman are perfectly good (and cheap). If you have problems with the main audio outputs (if the camera has any), it is also sometimes possible to output the sound from the headphone socket.

Input Levels

Cheaper cameras, and most analogue consumer formats, will not allow you the chance to adjust the input level coming in from the microphone. But if you can, don't ignore it. The input level has to be checked and adjusted before each take, no matter how fiddly the position of the level meters (one for each channel of input) and the dials. The worst thing is to have the levels constantly in the red - that means guaranteed distortion.

Sound Mixers (SQNs)

If you don't want to rely on the input levels of the camera, you can use a separate sound mixer (called an SQN) to preadjust the levels first. The SQN will be able to output a test signal (called 'tone') which you can use to set the input level of the camera to the appropriate position - after which, put gaffer tape over the dials to ensure they aren't jogged. The SQN should have XLR inputs and outputs as standard, a headphone socket, levels meters and dials.

Microphones

All cameras come with an on-board microphone. These are only good as back-up, because the mechanisms of the camera and handling noise are easily picked up, and also because the camera may simply be too far away from the subject to pick up good quality sound. But if your camera has no other sound inputs, then that's what you're going to be using.

If your camera has inputs, you can use a separate microphone. Microphones are defined by the method by which they pick up sound and the directionality of the sound they record.

• **Method** Two main ways exist to pick up sound - dynamic microphones or condenser microphones. Dynamic mikes use a mechanical process, and do not need batteries; condensers use an electrical process, and need on-board batteries (or 'phantom' power from a sound desk - if you're being loaned a condenser microphone from a musician or a recording studio, make sure they give you one that carries batteries).

• **Directionality** Hand mikes used by presenters and singers (like the ever durable SM58) are designed to pick up sound from in front of the microphone and partly from the sides in a sort of heart shape ('cardioid'). These are okay, but they do pick up extraneous noise from other directions. It's better to have a directional microphone which picks up sound from directly in front; these are long and thin in shape, usually mounted on a pistol grip, further enclosed within a cylinder and, in windy weather, a big furry sock. These are the microphones seen on professional film shoots mounted on the end of a long pole called a boom. Most media centres that hire video equipment should have one available for you to use (the Sennheiser 416 is the usual workhorse). If you can't get this, then a hand mike, a broom handle and some gaffer tape can make a substitute.

Radio mikes are useful when there is no other way of recording the sound. Maybe the angle is too wide, or the camera is moving so much that a boom would get in the way. The actor wears a tiny microphone concealed somewhere on their front, wired up to a transmitter hidden under their clothes. The sound recordist carries the receiver, which is plugged into the SQN or camera. They take time to put on, and are known for sometimes being more trouble than they're worth.

Recording Clean Dialogue

The job of the sound recordist is to record clean dialogue. Everything else - from the sounds of an explosion, to the sound of a car revving up, to the sound of a crowd in the background, to the minutest tinkle of glass hitting the floor - can be added in post-production. The sound recordist is well within their rights to ask for an extra take if something went wrong during a shot, no matter how good the actors' performances were. Things to watch out for include:

- Mumbled, incoherent or overlapping dialogue.
- Traffic noise - cars, trains, airplanes etc.
- The crew.
- Wind (atmospheric or otherwise).
- Radio mike interference or clothes rustling.
- Spectators shouting "cut!"

Sometimes you need sound going on in the background. People may be required to dance to music, in which case you need to be able to play it on set ('playback'); if there's dialogue during such a sequence, it's best to have playback when you start the shot so that the performers can get the rhythm, and switch off the music as soon as anyone is supposed to speak. If you have to shoot inside a moving car or any other environment which has continual sound, try and keep the mike as close to the performer as possible; radio mikes are especially useful here as they will always stay the same distance from the subject no matter the size of the shot.

Boom

One of the commonest errors seen in films is when the boom pokes into the shot. For this purpose, it's essential for whoever is holding the boom to ask for a frameline from the camera operator before the shot begins - simply a matter of putting the boom closer and closer to the subject until the camera operator says it's in shot. The boom can be held above, below, or level with the subject - just as long as it's pointed at the sound source. If there are several performers, this may involve some careful movement - the boom operator must make use of camera rehearsals to get this sorted out. The cable of the microphone should be twisted around the boom by spinning the pole and allowing the cable to wrap around it as you do so; a loose cable is at best annoying and at worst a hazard to life and limb.

Wildtracks & Atmos

Soundtracks are built up of many elements besides the dialogue, but you can save yourself time, stress and money in post-production by recording some of them on set. Specific sounds to be recorded are known as 'wildtracks' (they are 'wild' because they are not recorded at the same time as the picture). These may include the sound of a car engine, the bark of a dog, the scrape of a chair, an airplane landing, the background buzz of conversation in a pub; if you think you need something and it's available on set, get it while you have the opportunity. List the sounds you want along with your shotlist.

'Atmos' must be recorded in every room or location that you shoot in. This consists of everyone staying silent while the sound recordist gets 30 seconds of the background sound of the room. This is vital for sound continuity when you edit (see the Sound Editing chapter). For both atmos and wildtrack, the sound recordist should label the takes verbally since finding the material you want can be tricky when there are no visual cues.

Post-Production

Editing

Editing is the most important stage of making the film - this is the point at which it finally comes together. But good editing should not be calling attention to itself. The audience must remain unaware of the tricks that are being played upon them - because if they're aware of them, their attention is no longer on the story, and the story is the point of the whole thing.

Editing, on professional productions, is a collaboration between an editor and the director; the editor operates all the technology while the director supervises the process. You probably won't have this luxury when making a microbudget film, but it is helpful to have someone in with you or to have sat in with someone yourself.

Editing is the best place to learn about film-making. If you have access to a system for free, a good exercise is to take your favourite film and re-edit it to see how things can be changed. You'll learn some useful techniques, and maybe spot why the film's editor made the decisions he or she did in the first place.

Logging

The process of logging is not the most interesting - it's the sort of thing that TV companies delegate to work experience people - but it's absolutely vital to your edit. If you don't know where everything is, how are you going to put it in the film? Also logging can save you a lot of expensive hire charges by speeding up your edit or allowing you to batch digitise footage.

I do my logging at home. If the original footage is on a format that supports timecode, then I copy it onto VHS tapes with 'BITC' (Burnt-In Time-Code, pronounced "bitsy"). To get this, you need a VCR of the appropriate format with a video output labelled 'monitor' or 'super' on the back that outputs the video with the timecode superimposed on the picture. If the tape format doesn't have timecode, copy it to a format which does, and then copy those tapes to VHS as above. If that's not a possibility, use the timer on the VCR at home to give you a rough idea of where a shot is.

If you are batch digitising, make exact notes of where every shot begins and ends. If you're using a linear system, you probably only need to know where each shot begins. What's absolutely vital is knowing what was going on in each shot - what was intended, and the way it actually turned out; if an actor fluffed a line or if they did something particularly brilliant; if the lighting was slightly off; the size of the shot, and anything else you may notice. Forcing yourself to sit through the footage and getting to know it more intimately usually helps spark off ideas for the edit itself.

Paper Edit

To save time when working with expensive editing systems, you can make your decisions before you actually work with the pictures. So long as you have the footage logged, you can prepare a paper edit, possibly based upon the storyboard, making a list of which shots you need to use and in which order.

Offline & Online

Traditionally, video editing is divided into two stages: offline and online. These can be translated as 'rough cut' and 'final cut.' The offline stage is usually done on a cheaper system, so you can spend more time on it without bankrupting yourself. Then, for the final version of the film, the edit is recreated or adjusted on an online system. In linear editing, it's common to use two different tape formats for the two stages: for example, doing your rough cut on VHS, then the final cut on Betacam SP.

Computer editing has blurred this. The same system can be used for offline, sound mix and online; footage is digitised at a lower quality to begin with, the film is edited (with a sound mix if the system has the ability), and then the footage is redigitised at a higher quality to create a finished product which can be played out to tape. It's still possible, however, to do an offline on a cheap system with lower-resolution pictures, and then transfer that via an EDL (Edit Decision List) to another system with greater capabilities for an online.

No matter what system you're on, the first job is to edit the film together from beginning to end as you originally intended. This is the 'first assembly.' It may be a bit rough, and it will certainly be too long by at least a third, but now you can see what needs changing. Run it off onto a VHS and go away and watch it. Make notes. Work out what's wrong with it. Come

67

back with fresh ideas and re-edit it. Recut it again and again until you have it down to length. Let other people watch it and give their opinions, but exercise your judgement - not all the advice you get will be useful. Don't be precious about your camerawork; a shot that you love may be getting in the way of the scene. A lot of editing is about thinning down all the bits you love and selecting the ones that actually work. Once you've got a cut that you like, online it if you need to do things to it that need a better system, then master it to the best format you have available. Make a copy of this (called a 'dub') onto the same format, and then use this to make VHS copies if you need to - always preserve the master tape and use it as little as possible.

Editing With Coverage

If you've shot coverage, there's a simple way to get an edit of a scene and build up a first assembly quickly. Lay down the master shot first, then go back to the beginning of the scene and edit in the angles on individual characters or groups of characters, or any cutaways you may need. If you're working with a linear system, you'll find that, since performances are often slightly longer or shorter, timing may have slipped when you cut back to the master angle - you will need to re-record the master shot from that point onwards. On a non-linear system you can trim the shots down as necessary. This also works if you have only two angles on, for example, a conversation between two characters. Lay down one side of the conversation as a whole first, then insert the other side wherever it seems to be necessary to cut.

Shot Length

It doesn't take the eye long to get bored with a shot. If you give the audience a master angle to watch for a large part of the scene, attention can rapidly drop away. Similarly, a person speaking for longer than a few seconds doesn't need to be left on the screen all the time; reaction shots can be cut in. A little practise should give you a sense of when a shot has outstayed its welcome.

Transitions

Cutting from one scene to another may seem like a very simple business, but it offers enormous opportunities - and pitfalls. A common trick is to use dissolves, wipes, or a brief fade to black between scenes. These can quickly get tiresome, so use them sparingly, if at all. Their main use is for implying the passage of time.

When you cut to a new scene, the viewer needs a moment to realise where (and when) the new scene is taking place, particularly if the new location is unfamiliar. Therefore, it's common for scenes to begin on a wider shot before going in closer to concentrate on the subject. You can turn this on its head and conceal the nature of the location until later in the scene if you want to trick the audience for a moment - then use the reveal for a joke or a moment of insight.

Another nice thing to do is to make the images (or sounds) on either side of the cut have some relation to each other. You can do this to give information, keep the plot moving, or just for a nice visual moment. Some examples:

• Someone asks a question at the end of a scene. Someone, maybe even the same someone in the next scene - possibly years distant and thousands of miles away - answers it. (And thus the plot moves forward.)

• The camera ends a scene on a shot of a house. Cut to a shot of the house derelict, years later. (And thus we have been given information.)

• A character gets into a car and drives away. Cut to a shot of a child riding a tricycle before panning up to show the person waiting for the character in the car. (No actual plot or concrete information, but shots that have some common ground can be fun to play with.)

Of course, any of these can be played as their opposites, or used to trick the audience.

Match Action

One way to make cuts smoother is to cut on action. So long as the performer has been doing similar things in each take, you can cut from one shot in which, for example, a character is rising from a chair, to another angle where the character is completing the same action. Exact timing will need some work, but you can create the feeling of a smooth, single motion while cutting to a completely different angle or shot size.

Even if you don't have the same subject in frame, it's possible to cut on a common movement within the frame (remember the bone turning into a satellite in *2001: A Space Odyssey*?), or similar camera movement - or, of course, opposite movements (e.g. one person goes left; cut to another person going right. Or the camera tracks in; cut to a shot where the camera tracks out).

Cutting To Camera Movement

If you're not using Match Action, cutting to and from camera movement can be tricky. Cutting into the middle of a fast movement (or from a fast movement to a static frame) grabs the attention, and while this can be used effectively to draw the audience's interest, it may disrupt the flow of a scene if used haphazardly or in the wrong place. Cutting from one kind of movement to another can also be jarring, especially if the two movements are at substantially different speeds. If you want to cut to a movement, try cutting to it a frame or two before it begins, so that the eye has a better chance of going along with it.

Hard Cuts & Soft Cuts

Making a cut in both sound and picture at the same time is known as a 'hard cut,' and is rather abrupt. You'll be able to make smoother edits if you stagger the cuts on picture and sound. Say, for example, that you have a conversation between two people, during which you need to cut from one to the other. With hard cuts, you can only cut the picture between words or speeches, because the sound would otherwise be disrupted. Instead, try cutting from one character to another before they've finished speaking - but allow the sound of their speech to continue, and only cut to the sound from the second angle when the second character speaks. This is a 'soft cut,' which is less obvious to the viewer and gives you greater freedom to choose when to cut.

Extension/Compression Of Time

Time is rarely quite what it seems in films. It's possible to speed things up or slow them down to a tension-dripping crawl.

• **Compression** You can shorten scenes (and thus speed things up and prevent boredom) while still apparently showing a complete event. For example, a character has to walk from the middle of a room to a door. If you show them starting to walk, then a cutaway of someone watching, then them getting to the door, you can get the action done in a fraction of the time it would actually have taken.

• **Extension** The commonest example of this is the ticking clock scene, where something is about to explode, and we cut to and from the timer as the heroes make their frantic attempts to do something about it - but somehow, the timer takes twice as long to reach zero as the numbers ticking down would seem to indicate. Extending an action depends either on using cutaways to drag things out, or showing the same action repeated but from a different angle, or a combination of both.

Jump Cuts

It is possible, within a scene, to cut from a shot of one character to a similarly framed shot of the same character, but in which the character has moved position. Instead of seeing a continuity problem, the eye reads it as a brief jump in time. As such, it can be a great way to skip over dull moments in a performance. Violating reality in this way is jarring when done only once, but when it becomes a style - either throughout the film, or within a scene - the viewer accepts it readily.

Titles & Credits

Beginners have a tendency to create elaborate and lengthy opening title sequences, usually done to give the impression that this is a 'real' film. My advice is: don't bother. There's nothing that signals inexperience more than a long, dull title sequence on a short film. Just stick the title of the film up at the beginning in a simple way and get it over and done with - get to the story fast and hook your audience before they switch over.

Similarly, try and keep your credits short. Get everyone's name in, but don't drag them across the screen at a snail's pace. Fifteen to thirty seconds should be enough in most instances.

Linear/Non-Linear

There are two types of editing systems:

• **Linear** Uses two machines to copy shots from one tape onto another. It suffers from a serious difficulty: once an edit has been completed, it is impossible to add a shot or a scene somewhere in the middle without wiping over something that was there before.

• **Non-Linear** Works by 'digitising' the footage onto a computer, where it can be manipulated without the need for any of it to be copied over or destroyed. The editing is done on a timeline which graphically shows the sequence of shots. Most will allow you to manipulate the sound in the same way as the picture, and produce a reasonable sound mix. They should be able to play back digitised footage and the timeline on the screen, though more complicated effects will require the computer to do some 'rendering' before it can show you anything.

Scratch Editing

The easiest way to create a linear editing system is to connect your camera or a VCR to your VCR at home, and copy shots from one to the other. This, however, suffers from a few problems. Firstly, it's assemble editing (see the section below for details). Secondly, you cannot pre-set the points at which you can lay down a shot - you have to rely on your own timing to press the record and play buttons at the right moments.

Linear Suites

Linear systems are slowly dying out as everyone moves to non-linear, but many still exist. Media centres will usually have one or two available to hire, especially VHS systems which are good for practising on or doing an offline edit. Any tape format can be used to form a linear editing system - all you need is one player, one player/recorder and an edit controller which orders the VCRs about. The edit controller can function in one of two ways:

• **Assemble** editing is essentially the same thing as scratch editing, except that you can pre-select an exact 'in point' on both the source and destination tapes. An assemble edit will leave noise (the 'snow' you see on a blank tape) after it cuts if you have dropped a shot into the middle of some other footage; therefore you can only add shots onto the end of other shots.

• **Insert** editing allows you to add shots at any point, but only if a 'control track' exists on the tape (you have to record something on it - even a black screen will do). Assemble editing assumes that there is no control signal on the tape, and therefore it has no idea where exactly the frames begin and end - so it tramples all over the tape when it records. Insert editing works because a video signal is already present, and shots can be smoothly dropped in. Like assemble editing, you can select in points, but you can also have an out point which will allow you to cut the shot at the appropriate moment.

All linear suites with edit controllers allow you to preview an edit before you make it; always do this, just to be certain. Not all systems are exactly frame perfect when they cut, and some of them erase the in and out points you've programmed in when they do an edit, so make a note of what you intended if you need to make minor alterations.

More advanced linear suites will include another player to make it into a 3-machine suite. With the extra player, you can create cross-fades and wipes from one shot to another. It might also have a vision mixer, which will allow you to use video effects.

Non-Linear Suites

You will most likely be hiring (or borrowing) a system from a media centre or post-production house, but it's not impossible to buy a system and have it at home. Research the market before you part with your cash; a magazine called *Computer Video* publishes lists of currently available hardware and software with extensive information, and has a useful discussion board on its website. Play with a system before you buy it - find out for yourself what it can do. The various software packages you can use have many common features, but not all systems support every function - some need add-ons, and some are simply incapable. Check the system before you begin.

The first task is to copy footage from your tapes to 'media files' on the hard drive, a process known as 'digitisation.' Digitisation can be done 'on the fly,' simply pressing the relevant button to start and stop as the tape plays, or (if the tape format has timecode), you can type in the in point and out point and let the computer do it itself. 'Batch digitising' is a process whereby you give the information on multiple clips to the computer and leave it to digitise all of them, only changing tapes as necessary - useful if time or money are limited. Most systems allow you to digitise at different rates of compression; the more compressed a file is, the lower quality the image will be, but the less space it will take up. When doing your first assembly, digitise at the lowest quality possible to save space on the disks, since this will probably be in short supply. Later on, you can redigitise the material that survived into the final edit at higher quality. Some systems, which are based on digital-only video cards (which may not even accept analogue input!), can only digitise uncompressed footage, making disk space even more precious.

'Clips' of digitised material are stored in 'bins,' windows you can open on the screen to access the clips contained inside. Organise bins according to scenes, so that all the clips for a single scene can be found in the same place. If your film contains only one scene, create bins for each camera angle instead. When you go to add a clip to the timeline, you can usually select which part of the clip you want to lay down rather than having to add the whole thing and trim it later.

The timeline is where you actually do the work, laying down shot after shot. The workings of the timeline vary between the different software packages, but you should be able to both overlay shots on top of old material, or splice in shots, pushing aside the old material. You will also be able to trim or extend the beginning and end of every clip on the timeline to make adjustments.

Some systems support the 16:9 widescreen format, and can read anamorphic images correctly, but you'll have to make sure that the right option is selected. They will then show you the picture in the correct aspect ratio while still holding it in memory as an anamorphic image. When you output, you may get the option to convert the picture to a letter-box image which can be viewed on a standard 4:3 screen. Or you may not. If you want to use 16:9, make sure you find out what the system can and can't do.

Most non-linear systems will present you with a range of effects which you can use to modify your edit, so you may find yourself with an unexpected opportunity to make a cup of tea while the computer renders it. Some effects include:

- **Fades/Cross-Fades/Wipes**
- **Stills** Most systems allow you to specify a single frame of a clip or the timeline and make a still image of it - essentially another clip in which every frame is a copy of the original. You may also be able to import graphics files from outside and turn these into stills clips.
- **Titles** Most systems have some sort of titling facility, generally fairly basic, allowing for crawls and title rolls. Plug-in titling systems usually offer more choice and flexibility.
- **Colourisation** (Grading) Being able to change the amount of colour within a clip is a very useful tool; you might have pre-sets that allow you to make colour footage black and white, or sepia, or correct a shot where you forgot to white balance (but don't rely on this!).
- **Flips & Flops** Reversing the picture either horizontally or vertically can be useful if you've made a slight mistake with regards to the 180° rule. Beware of things that could give away the trick, like street names, newspapers and car number plates.
- **Slomo/Fastmo** Computers can speed up footage very easily, since all it does is cut out frames. Slowing down footage is more difficult. The computer will create 'in-between' frames to stretch out the footage, but the resulting image will still have a stepped quality. Some systems are better at this than others.
- **Film Look** Every video frame (25 per second) is made up of two interlaced 'fields,' effectively meaning that video runs at 50 frames a second. Film, however, only has one field per frame; some systems can emulate this by doubling up on the fields within a video frame. There's more to film look than this, but it's a start.

A non-linear system should give you two tracks of audio to play with (i.e. stereo), and most will allow more. However, there are often limitations on how many you can play out at once. They are manipulated in much the same way as video tracks, with the exception that you may be able to change volume, pan, EQ or other settings. A useful feature, if you have it, is 'audio scrub,' which allows you to drag the mouse across an audio clip at any speed and hear a frame or so of the audio at pre-set intervals, so you get a sort of sampling of the audio every time you move the mouse up or down the timeline.

The edit is saved as a complete 'project,' incorporating the current timeline and state of clips and bins. This is not transferable between different software packages, but you should have the option to produce an Edit Decision List (EDL), which is a text file containing basic information about the edit. This can be imported to another system and used as the basis to redigitise the necessary footage. This is useful if you need to go to another system, or to save memory, since EDL files are very small.

Playing the final edit out onto tape is a simpler matter on some systems than others. Some allow you to watch the edit on a monitor as it plays, and you can therefore plug in a VCR and record it at the same time. Others find this a bit of a stretch, and require that you render the whole edit (usually labelled as 'Make Movie') before you can play it all back in one go.

Preroll

When a tape recorder is ordered by a linear or non-linear system to play a piece of footage, it doesn't start at the beginning. It nips back to a few seconds before that point, and then starts playing, in order to get the player up to speed and working smoothly. However, if your timecode is discontinuous, the system may become confused and get trapped rewinding and fast-forwarding to find a non-existent timecode. You can also get this problem if the required material is too close to the beginning of a tape (so always record 20 seconds of nonsense when putting a new tape in the camera). Some systems allow you to reduce preroll time in order to solve these problems, and a non-linear suite may allow you to digitise 'on the fly' without needing to look up the timecode; but sometimes the problem can be insoluble without copying the material to another tape.

Sound Editing

Sound can enhance your picture edit, make cuts smoother, introduce tension where there was none, make an unreal environment suddenly pulse with life - but it's harder work. The ear is better able to detect mistakes and discontinuity than the eye. The eye can be switched off by shutting the eyelids, and suffers no feelings of discontinuity if you quickly flick them from side to side. But the ears cannot be switched off, nor are they directional in the same way that eyes are. Creating sound continuity within a scene is vital for preserving the illusion of reality and, along with a clearly audible dialogue track, is the most basic aspect of sound editing to get right.

When you edit you need to create these tracks:

- **Dialogue** A clean dialogue track is essential. No background noise, all lines as audible as possible. You may need to re-record some lines (see ADR, below).
- **Sound Effects**
- **Temp Music** Anything you grab from your CD collection to edit the picture to and give a composer a guide. If you're not distributing, or if the copyright is easily gained, this can even be your final music track
- **Atmos** In every scene, lay down a continuous track of the atmos you recorded for the scene. This will cover any gap or dodgy cut in the other tracks and preserve sound continuity

These must, where possible, be kept separate to prevent confusion and mistakes. On a professional production, these tracks will be taken to a specialised dubbing studio for mixing once the picture edit is complete. Naturally, this is hideously expensive. You will be much more likely to be mixing your sound with whatever equipment is available; linear suites often have a sound desk that you can route sound through and adjust as it goes, and non-linear suites should have built-in options to work on the sound. Some important things you should be able to do are:

- **Echo (Repeat) And Reverb** Sound has a habit of bouncing off hard surfaces and reflecting back to be heard again. This can create echoes, which can be reproduced electronically. In film, echoes are generally limited to psychological effects and simulating the effect when you couldn't get it on location. A more important result of sound bouncing off surfaces is 'reverb.' In a more enclosed environment, sound bounces so close to the source that the repeated sound is neither distinct nor separate from the original sound; we hear the sound seem to continue for a time. This effect can be best observed by going into a church and clapping, then going out into the open air and doing so again - note how much longer the sound carries on inside the church. Every kind of room has its own sound quality. Soft surfaces absorb sound; hard surfaces reflect it. The kind of furniture or the number of people in a room can change the quality of the reverb. If your sound is recorded on location, then it's usually fine. But additional sound effects, ADR or background music (music heard by the actors in the scene), must be matched to the kind of sound you had on location.

- **EQ** Stands for 'Equalisation,' and is the system whereby the different frequencies of sound within a track can be made louder or quieter as you wish. Sound is made up of vibrations in the air; the more vibrations there are per second, the higher pitched we perceive the sound to be. For practical purposes, the useful range is 80Hz to 12kHz. Outside of this, sound can be heard, but only barely. A trumpet can range between 200 and 800Hz, and a human soprano voice goes from about 250Hz to 1.2kHz. You may have EQ controls that can only change the levels of a pre-selected range of frequencies, or you may be able to select the frequency to be adjusted. These controls can usually be found inside non-linear editing systems, and for linear systems, on the sound desk that comes with the system (if there is one). If, for example, you want to make a voice sound like it's coming through a telephone, cut off everything below 150Hz and above 3.6kHz.

• **Compression/Normalisation** Sound levels from dialogue have a tendency to vary a great deal during any given speech, and a 'compressor' can smooth out the loud and quiet bits. This makes the voice seem closer and more intimate, very useful for things like whispering and voice-overs. Computers may be able to 'normalise' a sound file or a clip within a non-linear editing system; this brings quiet bits up and turns the loud bits down.

• **Stereo** Stereo works by taking advantage of the fact that we hear with two ears. A sound coming equally from both speakers will be perceived as coming from a point in-between the two. Many cameras will record in stereo through their on-board microphones, and all non-linear editing systems will give you pairs of audio tracks so you can preserve stereo effects. You should be able to pan the sound between the two speakers so that it appears to come from the left, the right, or anywhere in-between. When you have two characters talking to each other, panning one to the left and one to the right will help to delineate them. Moving a sound from one side to another (especially if the source in the film is moving) is a good way to call attention to it. Dolby Stereo is the system of encoding sound for cinema or video/DVD distribution. Although a Dolby license is free for films under 40 minutes, you will need to have your sound mixed at a Dolby-capable studio, which will cost you an arm, a leg, and most of your major intestines. So if you do eventually make a film print of your work, it's likely that it's going to be mono, with all the audio coming out of the central speaker and sounding muddy.

ADR (Automated Dialogue Replacement)

If sync sound wasn't recorded on location, or the actor's voice was indistinct, then they (or someone else) can be called in to re-record the dialogue. This new dialogue track is pasted back into the soundtrack, with effects added to make it match the original dialogue as far as is possible. This is also known as 'looping.'

You can do some cheap ADR by plugging in a microphone and getting the actors to record their lines in time to the edit. You digitise the audio coming in while playing a copy of the edit on a VHS. One problem is that 'plosive' sounds (e.g. Ps and Bs) tend to be very loud and cause a 'pop' on the recording. To stop this, try putting a 'pop shield' between the performer and microphone - a pair of tights stretched between a ring of a few inches diameter will do.

Changing Settings Over Time

You will probably want to be able to adjust settings as the story progresses - slowly raising the volume of a character as they get more incensed, panning objects going left to right rather than leaving them in one place, changing the EQ levels for a piece of music as the characters progress from outside the club to inside.

Fully-equipped dubbing studios come with sound desks which motorise the knobs and faders to repeat every action. The sound desks in linear editing suites are unlikely to come with this function. When you make your edits, you must adjust the sound desk manually as you go. Practise with it in preview first. Bear in mind that once the sound is laid down, you won't be able to change it back; only attempt this if you have no intention or option of mixing the sound separately later.

Non-linear systems usually give you the opportunity to adjust things like volume, pan, EQ and others over the course of the track. They may give you a panel with virtual faders to play with, or show the settings graphically on the timeline.

Shareware

If you don't have access to the above kinds of effects, but are capable of turning your audio into computer files and have a reasonable sound card in your computer, you can look on the Internet for shareware programs that will do wonderful things to your sound. Programs exist to do just about everything from a simple compression effect, to making an actor sound like they are on helium.

Foley & Sound FX

There are three ways to add sound effects to augment your soundtrack: record them on location, copy them from a sound effects (fx) album, or record during post-production.

Effects recorded specifically for a production are known as 'foley,' 'footsteps' or 'spot effects.' Recording a sound effect is a fairly easy thing to do, but takes skill and a surprising amount of time and effort (or money) to get right if it isn't the actual sound recorded on location.

For those of us with less skill or money to spend, there are CDs available which contain vast numbers of sound effects. Some of these are available in music shops, but they are not copyright-free. The real ones are usually only available by mail order, and tend to cost more (about £30 each), but the extra money pays for copyright clearance.

If you do not intend to send the piece for distribution, have a look through your film collection for sounds that seem appropriate and are clean - this is a good way to get things like unusual atmos sounds like foreign cities and strange environments.

The Internet is also a source for sound effects, but not quite as useful as you might think. Online sound effects libraries are usually cut-down versions designed to sell CDs. Sound quality may be deliberately degraded to dissuade people from actually using the fx - but still, you can sometimes find just the thing you're looking for.

Drawing Attention

Sound can help to draw attention to a particular object, person or event in the film, just by having it a little louder than everything else. Similarly, you can de-emphasise something if you wish to. For example, if a character's attention wanders, reduce the volume of the person talking to them. The audience will understand what's going on without needing to be told.

Semi-Detached Sound

Sound doesn't need to come from within the frame. You can often use a sound effect to signify that something has happened, particularly if you're making a comedy. Nor does sound have to be the exact appropriate noise for any given moment - you can do a lot of comedy by using inappropriate sound effects. An entire soundtrack can be built up of sound not recorded on location; you can get sound effects and atmos from CDs, and record music and dialogue in a studio if you want to.

Noise & Silence

A quiet soundtrack can work just as powerfully as a loud one. If a character is creeping down a sewer with gun in hand, loud noises all around would be a waste when you could have just the atmos from the scene, a few quiet footsteps to go with the character, and then the squeal of a rat when the character reacts to a noise. A sudden sound appearing at such a moment of tension can be devastating.

Music

Uses & Styles

'Background' music is music heard by the characters. It will have to be carefully adjusted to make it sound like it's being played in the appropriate location; music heard outside a nightclub, for example, will have to be EQed so all that remains is the thumping lower registers. Organ music from a cathedral will need reverb. One problem is that the recording quality of most music is so high that it may put the sound you recorded on location to shame: when you add music, it may sound more real than the dialogue of the characters speaking. You will usually need to take out some of the lower frequencies in order to make the sound just that little bit tinnier than the voices in the room, making it sound more like it's coming from a source somewhere in the location.

Sound not heard by the characters is known as 'incidental' or 'featured' music. This has a multitude of uses, from the big movie that plasters a lush orchestral score everywhere, to the art-house flick with a single recurring theme that pops up sparingly. The main purpose of music is to assist with the emotional delivery of any given scene.

Music can also be useful to mask problems. The continuity of music will tend to smooth out jagged edges, change the tone of a scene, or speed it up, or slow it down. And never underestimate the power of letting the music suddenly stop; a great tension getter.

Composing & Recording

The reason to go to a composer rather than your CD collection is because the composer (and the relevant musicians, if any) will own the copyright to the work and (hopefully) be willing to let you use it without cost. Be honest with your composer about what you need for the music. Tell them as early as possible. If you can, let them in on the editing process so they can see what you're up to. Once you have the picture edit locked down, go through the film scene by scene and discuss what it needs in terms of music. Give them a reasonable amount of time - a few weeks at least. They should be able to deliver the music on CD, DAT or MiniDisc.

Contact local media centres to see if they include recording studio facilities; there you may get hold of relevant contacts. Community-based recording studios may also have what you're looking for. Universities often have student music societies where you can find musicians. Local bands may be glad of a chance to put their music on a film. It's probably easier to work with a composer who has access to recording equipment, and the keyboards and sequencers needed to put together a soundtrack from scratch.

Copyright

If you are hoping to take your films to festivals and maybe get a TV sale, you will need to have the rights to do so. This can be surprisingly easy, especially if the music concerned is not chart music or particularly popular. The MCPS (Mechanical Copyright Protection Society) will tell you who currently owns the recording rights of the music, and how much you will be charged for using it (make sure you say what kind of distribution you are intending). If this figure seems a little too large, you can go directly to the owners of the recording and compositional rights (who may very well be different people) and ask very nicely if they'll let you have the music for free for such and such distribution. Festival rights can often be obtained, but TV or theatrical rights are unlikely. If they do agree, make sure you get it in writing as you may need to prove it.

Library music is different. A number of companies produce CDs full of music just so that you can use them in productions, without the hassle of composing or recording it yourself. The drawback is that it has to be paid for if you use it. Payments are collected by the MCPS, with whom you must register (for free) before you can actually begin to seek a license to use the music. A minute of music for festival distribution will eat up the best part of a hundred quid, so it's not a cheap shortcut.

Distribution

Know Your Audience

Who do you want to make films for? Teenagers? Professionals? Under fives? OAPs? Men? Women? Don't assume that everyone will get your film, or even want to. In making short films, you are relatively lucky - the audience is so small that it will get watched mainly by the sort of people who watch short films. But out in the real world, millions are spent on 'positioning' films so that the target audience will realise that the film is aimed at them. While some films will have a universal appeal, most will be making certain assumptions about what the audience knows and understands. *Trainspotting*, for example, was clearly not intended for older people. Being aware of having a particular audience, and knowing what they can cope with and what they expect, will help enormously in both keeping your film coherent and in selling it.

Delivery Stuff

- **Stills** If you want to sell a film, you absolutely must have a good selection of stills, preferably both black and white and colour. Frame grabs aren't enough. Professional photographers are usually expensive, so get a friend to do this, using an SLR camera rather than a compact. You need shots which tell the story and set up the main characters. What you don't need are shots of the crew doing their jobs or arsing about.

- **Music List** To avoid getting sued by the owners of the music, everyone who might distribute your film will want a list of music used, along with who owns it, and an assurance that you have gained the rights necessary.

- **Tapes** You'll have to provide tapes. Standard procedure is to send a VHS copy as your application, and some will be able to use this for presentation as well, but not many - usually only small film clubs. Most will require some sort of broadcast quality tape, though the definition of broadcast quality varies. Beta SP or Digibeta are normal.

- **Video Cover** It helps if your video has a nice cover. People are a little more likely to pick up an attractive piece of packaging than they are to pick up something with a photocopy stuck in the cover. But don't get hung up on it; use a simple, expressive visual idea which gives the hook of the story. Get to know programs like QuarkXpress and Photoshop and put together something tasteful and simple, rather than something cluttered and shouty.

Festivals & Competitions

Festivals are places to be seen and inform the industry that you have arrived. The right film in the right festival in the right screening seen by the right individual can change your life overnight. Or at least, that's the theory. The reality is that short film festivals are chock full of shorts all competing for attention and most of them don't get very much. On the other hand, it's a good way to test the waters and see what an audience actually thinks of your film when it's up on a big screen. You may be pleased with their reactions and you may be horrified, but you'll certainly learn something.

Some of these festivals are competitive, and give out awards. Getting an award is a great experience, though not necessarily a life-changing event. Many of the awards on offer won't cause a single batting of an eyelid within the industry. But it's good to have on your CV.

The best thing you can do at festivals is network. Find out who people are and what they do, and make them aware of who you are and what you can do. Get to know how the industry is structured and what might be expected of you. See who's interested in your work and wants to get to know it better. Find the people at your level or a little above who you can get experience from by helping. Find people whom you can give experience by allowing them to help you.

In this country, Brief Encounters (Bristol, November), the British Short Films Festival (London, September), the Edinburgh International Film Festival (August) and many others accept shorts. The *BFI Handbook* lists film festivals, as does the *Guerrilla Film-Maker's Handbook*, and if you go to www.netribution.co.uk and sign up, you will get a monthly email newsletter which lists upcoming festival deadlines (among many other useful things). There are, of course, a number of international festivals which you can apply to, most with bilingual application forms. Alternatively, the British Council have a department dedicated to sending films out to international festivals, including shorts.

TV

Theoretically, all channels are open to submissions, but terrestrial channels tend to show films they have made themselves or bought in from abroad. You're much more likely to make a sale to one of the non-terrestrial channels such as FilmFour or Sky Moviemax. FilmFour in particular are dedicated to showing short films in the gaps between their main programming, and are willing to pay. Of course, if your short film is particularly suited to the theme of an individual channel, you will have a much greater chance of a speculative sale.

If you sell your film to TV, you'll need to provide a broadcast quality copy and sign a contract which will probably mean giving up all TV rights to it for a number of years, in territories which, apart from the UK, may include Eire and the whole of Europe. The money is unlikely to remunerate you fully for all the time and effort you put into it, but the main thing is the kudos of getting a TV screening.

Cinema

Cinema distribution is limited, but some attempts are being made to match shorts up with features, just as in the old days. The catch with cinema distribution is that you have to have the film transferred to 35mm, and usually pay for it yourself. It's an expensive process which is difficult to get discounted down to microbudget levels. Also, ten minutes is the absolute maximum length that is accepted, and shorter is definitely better in this case. Payment is likely to be non-existent. A cinema release is better for your reputation than your pocket.

Internet

Probably the easiest way to get your film distributed, and the widest audience you are likely to find, is on the Internet. Since it takes so long to download video, the Internet is a medium where the shorter type of film has come into its own. Sites that show short films are appearing all the time, and plenty of well-established broadcasters and portals are also getting in on the act. Several companies also list the films in order of how popular they are, so you can get an idea of whether or not the audience actually likes your film. For the Internet, you will probably be asked to sign over non-exclusive Internet rights - non-exclusive because the idea of exclusivity on the Internet is a bit bizarre. If you already have a TV sale, they may put it on their website and pay you a bit extra as well. You will normally have to deliver the film on broadcast quality videotape. The company will have the film transferred and encoded themselves.

References

Contacts

Media Centres

This isn't a complete list - if there's nothing in your part of the country, contact your Regional Arts Board (if you're in England), Media Development Agency or National Film Agency (if you're in Scotland, Wales and Northern Ireland) to see if there's one nearby.

Connections, Palingswick House, 241 King Street, London W6 9LP tel: 020 8741 1766

Depot Studios, Bond Street, Coventry CV1 4AH tel: 024 7652 5074

Edinburgh Film Workshop Trust, 29 Albany Street, Edinburgh EH1 3QN tel: 0131 557 5242

Exeter Phoenix New Media Centre, Bradninch Place, Gandy Street, Exeter EX4 3LS tel: 01392 667066

Film House/Ty Ffilm, Chapter Arts Centre, Market Road, Canton, Cardiff CF5 1QE tel: 01222 409990

Four Corners Film Workshop, 113 Roman Road, Bethnal Green, London E2 OQN tel: 020 8981 6111

Glasgow Film And Video Workshop, 3rd Floor, 34 Albion Street, Merchant City, Glasgow G1 1LH tel: 0141 553 2620

Hull Time Based Arts, AvidLAB, 8 Posterngate, Hull HU1 2JN tel: 01482 586340

Intermedia Film And Video, 19 Heathcoat Street, Nottingham NG1 3AF tel: 0115 955 6909

Light House, The Chubb Buildings, Fryer St, Wolverhampton WV1 1HT tel: 01902 716055

Lighthouse Brighton Media Centre, 9 -12 Middle Street, Brighton BN1 1AL tel: 01273 384222

Line Out, Fosse Arts Centre, Mantle Road, Leicester LE3 5HG tel: 0116 262 1265

Lux, Lux Building, 2-4 Hoxton Square, London N1 6NU tel: 020 7684 0101/0202

Media Arts Town Hall Studios, Regent Circus, Swindon SN1 1QF tel: 01793 463226

Mersey Film And Video, 13-15 Hope Street, Liverpool L1 9BQ tel: 0151 708 5259

Nerve Centre, 2nd Floor, Northern Counties Building, 8 Customs House Street, Derry BT48 6AE tel: 028 7926 0562

Northern Visions, 4 Lower Donegal Street Place, Belfast BT1 2FN tel: 028 9024 5495

Picture This Moving Image, Spike Island Studios, Sydney Row, Bristol BS1 6UU tel: 0117 925 7010

Sheffield Independent Film, 5 Brown Street, Sheffield S1 2BS tel: 0114 272 0304

Signals Essex Media Centre, Victoria Chambers, St Runwald Street, Colchester C01 1HF tel: 01206 560255

Vivid, Unit 311F, The Big Peg, 120 Vyse Street, Birmingham B18 6ND tel: 0121 233 4061

WFA Media And Cultural Centre, 9 Lucy Street, Manchester M15 4BX tel: 0161 848 9782/5

Miscellaneous

British Council, Films Department, 11 Portland Place, London W1N 4EJ tel: 0207 389 3065 fax: 0207 389 3041 - www.britishcouncil.org/arts/film/bc.htm - Distributes British shorts overseas.

Film Council, 10 Little Portland Street, London W1W 7JG tel: 020 7861 7861 fax 020 7861 7862 - www.filmcouncil.org.uk

Mechanical Copyright Protection Society (MCPS), Elgar House, 41 Streatham High Road, London SW16 1ER tel: 0208 769 4400/0208 664 4400 fax: 0208 769 8792 - www.mcps.co.uk

New Producers' Alliance (NPA), 9 Bourlet Close, London W1RP 7PJ tel: 0207 580 2480 fax: 0207 580 2484 - www.npa.org.uk - Independent producers' organisation.

Short Film Bureau, 47 Poland Street, London, W1F 7NB tel: 0207 734 8708 fax: 0207 734 2406 - www.shortfilmbureau.com - Distributors of cinema shorts.

Spotlight, 7 Leicester Place, London WC2H 7BP tel: 0207 437 7631 fax: 0207 437 5881 - www.spotlightcd.co.uk - Catalogue of UK actors. Phone line gives details of agents.

Women In Film & Television, Garden Studios, 11/15 Betterton Street, London WC 2H 9BP tel: 0207 379 0344 fax: 0207 379 2413 - www.wftv.org.uk

Websites

Atom Films - www.atomfilms.com - Online film distribution. Watch films!

Drew's Script-o-Rama - www.script-o-rama.com - A collection of film scripts to download.

Exposure - www.exposure.co.uk - Excellent low-budget film-making site. Features the Complete Eejit's Guide To Film-Making, a huge compendium of advice, tricks and tips.

Filmfestivalspro.com - www.filmfestivalspro.com - provides listings of film festivals by application deadline date.

Netribition Film Network - www.netribution.co.uk - Film-makers' web magazine, also comes in email form.

Peeping Tom's Film Club - www.geocities.com/SoHo/Studios/8451/index2.htm - Excellent site for microbudget/indie/underground cinema.

Shooting People - www.shootingpeople.org - Email newsletter for film-makers. Also has a separate screenwriter's version. Indispensable.

Periodicals

Broadcast, 33-39 Bowling Green Lane, London EC1R 0DA tel: 0207 505 8014 - Weekly journal of the television industry.

Computer Video, 57-59 Rochester Place, London NW1 9JU tel: 020 7331 1000 fax: 020 7331 1241 - www.computervideo.net - Monthly magazine for editing systems.

Creation, 3rd Floor, 30-31 Islington Green, London N1 8DU tel: 0207 226 8586 - Coverage of Film & TV industry aimed at indie film-makers.

Filmwaves, PO Box 420, Edgware HA8 0XA tel: 0208 906 4794 - www.users.global-net.co.uk/~filmwave - Underground & microbudget magazine.

Production & Casting Report (PCR), PO Box 11, London N1 7JZ tel: 0207 566 8282 fax: 0207 566 8284 - Weekly newsletter for acting opportunities. Ads can be placed for free.

Screen International, 33-39 Bowling Green Lane, London EC1R 0DA tel: 0207 505 8056 fax: 0207 505 8116 - Weekly journal of the international film industry.

Books

The Guerrilla Film-Makers' Handbook (2nd Edition) by Chris Jones & Genevieve Jolliffe, Continuum Publishing Group, 639 Pages, £19.99, ISBN 0826447139 - www.livingspirit.com - Pretty much everything you need to know about anything. It's not a handbook; it's a bible.

Lowdown: The Low-Budget Funding Guide, by Chris Chandler, The Film Council, free or at www.filmcouncil.org.uk/film-makers/lowdown/ - Pamphlet on low-budget film-making, issued every year. Gives info and advice on all funding schemes in the UK, and lots of contact information.

Getting Into Films & Television by Robert Angell and David Puttnam, How To Books, 1999, 188 Pages, £9.99, ISBN 1857035453 - Careers in the industry.

Story by Robert McKee, Methuen Publishing Company, 1999, 477 Pages, £12.99, ISBN 0413715604 - About the most comprehensive and yet the most flexible explanation of how stories work that I know of.

Screenplay by Syd Field, Bantam Doubleday Dell Publishing Group, 1998, 262 Pages, £11.00, ISBN 0440576474 - Another excellent examination of the screenwriter's craft, though more dogmatic about the three-act structure and Hollywood style.

How To Make Money Scriptwriting (2nd Edition), by Julian Friedmann, Intellect Books, 2000, 224 pages, £14.99, ISBN 184150002X - About the only book on the British screenwriting market, with some interesting observations on the craft of writing.

Production Safety For Film, Television And Video by Robin Small, Focal Press, 1998, 224 Pages, £19.99, ISBN 0240515315 - Comprehensive guide to health and safety.

BFI Film & Television Handbook 2001 by Eddie Dyja, BFI, 2000, 432 Pages, £20.00, ISBN 0851708188 - The basic contacts book for the British film and television industries. Reissued every year.

The Media Guide 2001, Edited by Steve Peak and Paul Fisher, Fourth Estate, November 2000, £4.99, ISBN 1841154237 - The Guardian's contacts book for everything to do with the media and journalism. Invaluable for producers as it contains the official contact info for everything. Reissued every year.

Adventures In The Screen Trade by William Goldman, Abacus, 1996, 432 Pages, £9.99, ISBN 034910705X - Goldman tells the tale of his life in films and the lowly status that writers have to live with. A great read, though not a technical screenwriting book.

Rebel Without A Crew by Robert Rodriguez, Faber and Faber, 1996, 296 Pages, £12.99, ISBN 057117891X - Rodriguez' diaries from the production of *El Mariachi* (made with $7,000 and shot in a little town in Mexico) and what followed. Includes a Ten-minute Film School.

Lighting For Television And Film by Gerald Millerson, Focus Press, 1999, 466 Pages, £24.99, ISBN 024051582X - Basic textbook on lighting.

Films About Film-Making

These films show the actual production process in one way or another. (This is not a complete list by any stretch of the imagination.) In addition, you will find that most DVD releases of films contain interesting background info on how they were made; for example, the dual DVD of *El Mariachi* and *Desperado* (both Dir: Robert Rodriguez) is excellent.

American Movie (Dir: Chris Smith, 1999) - Documentary about Mark Borchardt, desperately trying to make a horror film with any and every means at his disposal.

Boogie Nights (Dir: Paul Thomas Anderson, 1997) VHS: EVS1247, £5.99, VHS Widescreen: EVS1290, £15.99, DVD: EDV9004, £13.99, 149 mins, Cert 18 - A young man with an enviable asset makes his way into the world of porno films.

Ed Wood (Dir: Tim Burton, 1994) VHS: CC7842, £5.99, 121 mins, Cert 15 - Biopic about the 'worst director in history,' who was nevertheless very inventive in finding funding.

Le Confessional (Dir: Robert LePage, 1995) VHS: ART136, £15.99, 97 mins, Cert 15 - A man searches for his brother in the present, while flashbacks tell the story of his ancestors in Quebec City while Alfred Hitchcock was in town shooting *I Confess*.

Le Mépris (Dir: Jean-Luc Godard, 1963) VHS: CR211 , £15.99, 99 mins, Cert 15 - A Frenchman loses his girlfriend to an American producer who is making a film with legendary director Fritz Lang.

Living In Oblivion (Dir: Tom DiCillo, 1995) VHS: EVS1203, £13.99, 94 mins, Cert 15 - On the set of a low-budget feature the cast and crew fight, bitch and bicker their way through a typical day's work.

Man Bites Dog (Dir: Rémy Belvaux/André Bonzel/Benoit Poelvoorde, 1992) VHS: TVT1074, £15.99, DVD: TVD3308, £19.99, 92 mins, Cert 18 - A documentary crew follow a serial killer as he goes about his daily 'work.'

Peeping Tom (Dir: Michael Powell, 1960) VHS: S038187, £10.99, 96 mins, Cert 18 - A lowly technician at a British film studio obsesses about making films and watching people - to the point where he murders them as he films them.

Sunset Boulevard (Dir: Billy Wilder, 1950) VHS: VHR4295, £10.99, 105 mins, Cert PG - A failed screenwriter is trapped into fuelling the comeback fantasies of a faded silent-film star.

The Player (Dir: Robert Altman, 1992) VHS: 0432583, deleted - A Hollywood exec receives death threats as he goes about his daily business, turning down pitches from screenwriters.

Visions Of Light (Dir: Arnold Glassman/Todd McCarthy/Stuart Samuels, 1992) VHS: CAV022, £15.99, 90 mins, Cert PG - Inspirational documentary about cinematography, with examples from the whole history of cinema.

Volere Volare (Dir: Maurizio Nichetti, 1991) VHS: TVT29, £15.99, 91 mins, Cert 18 - An Italian foley artist slowly turns into a cartoon version of himself as he pursues the woman he loves.

Glossary

180° Rule - A fundamental rule of camerawork. You must not cut to a point on the other side of an imaginary line between two characters. Aka **Crossing The Line**.

2-Machine Suite - A **Linear Editing** suite with two VCRs: a player and recorder. It cannot perform **Transitions** like **Fades** and **Wipes**.

2-Shot - A shot with two people in the **Frame**.

3-Machine Suite - A **Linear Editing** suite with three VCRs: two players and a recorder. It can perform **Transitions** like **Fades** and **Wipes**.

ADC - Analogue to Digital Converter. A device which turns an **Analogue** signal into a **Digital** one. See **DAC**.

ADR - Automated Dialogue Replacement. A system of re-recording dialogue in **Post-Production** if the original dialogue is faulty.

Analogue - Any recording system which records video or audio as waveforms. Subject to **Generation Loss**. See also **Digital**.

Anamorphic - An anamorphic process, electronic or optical, squeezes a **Widescreen** image into a **Fullscreen** shape, and unsqueezes it later. When squeezed, people and objects seem very tall and thin.

Aperture/Iris - The opening between the **Lens** and the receptors (**CCDs**), which is used to control how much light is coming into the camera. Also affects **Depth of Field**.

Aspect Ratio - The ratio of the horizontal edge of the screen to the vertical edge - e.g. a standard **Fullscreen** TV is 4:3, and a **Widescreen** TV is 16:9.

Assemble Editing - A form of **Linear Editing** which does not use a **Control Track**. Shots can only be laid down one after another.

Assistant Director - Member of the crew responsible for running the set.

Atmos - Background noise recorded to assist continuity when mixing the soundtrack.

Audio Scrub - A feature on **Non-Linear Editing** systems which allows audio to be monitored as a pointer is pulled across the **Timeline**.

Autofocus - A feature on a camera which automatically adjusts the focus. Can be very unpredictable and problematic to use for drama.

Available Light - Light sources already available in a location, e.g. the sun or street lamps.

Back Light - A light shining from behind the subject, sometimes called a 'Hair Light'; an element of **Three-Point Lighting**.

Background Action - The actions of extras; a cue given to extras to begin before the cast.

Background Music - Music heard in a scene by characters.

Balanced Leads - Balanced audio leads (**XLRs**, aka **Cannons**) are protected against unwanted radio interference; **Unbalanced** audio leads (**Phonos**, **Jacks**, **Minijacks**) are vulnerable over distances of a few metres or more.

Ballast - A power transformer that comes with a **Daylight Balanced Light** such as an **HMI** or **MSR**.

Barn Doors - The four flaps on the front of a light which can be used to cut down or control light, and also hang **Gels** or **Diffusers** from.

Barney - A light camera covering which protects from rain and minimises camera noise.

Batch Digitising - A process on **Non-Linear Editing** systems in which the computer automatically digitises footage based upon logging information.

BCU - Big Close-Up. A shot size that shows the middle portion of the face.

Bin - A folder in a **Non-Linear Editing** program which contains **Clips**.

BITC - Burnt-In TimeCode. A **Timecode** display on video which is part of the picture and cannot be removed.

Blimp - A casing for the camera which blocks camera noise.

Blocking - A rehearsal process in which the movements of actors (and camera) around the set are planned out.

Blonde - A 2000 watt (2kW) **Tungsten** light without a **Fresnel** lens.

BNC - A coaxial video cable (not the same as a TV aerial cable!) commonly used on professional equipment.

Boom - A pole upon which a microphone is mounted.

Broadcast Quality - Video which meets the standards for television broadcast. Betacam, DVCAM, DVCPro and Digital S formats usually qualify, but standards vary.

Bubble - Common term for a light bulb used in professional film lights.

Business - Physical actions performed by actors, often added during rehearsal.

Buzz Track - See **Atmos**.

Cable Bashing - The task of keeping cables leading from a moving camera or microphone out of harm's way.

Call Sheet - A daily information sheet including the day's schedule, special arrangements, weather, contact information etc.

Camera Tape - White tape (similar to electrician's tape) which can be written on and used for labelling.

Cannon - aka **XLR**. A **Balanced** audio lead.

CCD - **C**harge **C**ouple **D**evice. A light receptor in a camera. 3CCD means that three receptors are used, one for each of the three primary colours - red, green and blue. See **Component**.

Clapperboard - aka **Slate**. The board placed in front of a film camera before a shot, used to identify it and provide a cue for synching up sound in post-production.

Clip - A piece of footage; a video/audio/audio-visual file on a **Non-Linear Editing** system.

Clone - A copy of video or audio which has been transferred by a **Digital** process and therefore has suffered no **Generation Loss**. See **Dubbing**.

Colour Temperature - The temperature of a light source; important as some lights which seem white to human eyes may seem blue or orange to a camera. Measured in **Kelvins**.

Colourisation - Changing colour levels in footage with video equipment. See **Grading**.

Component - A video signal split into the three primary colours (red, green, blue) and carried upon three separate leads. Provides a higher-quality picture. See **Composite**.

Composite - A video signal carried upon a single lead. See **Component**.

Compressor - An effects box in a **Dubbing Studio** which controls incoming audio levels by setting limits upon a signal. Can help to make voices sound very nearby and intimate.

Condenser Microphone - A microphone that uses an electrical process to pick up sound. Requires **Phantom Power** either from batteries or a sound desk, and is more fragile than a **Dynamic Microphone**.

Control Track - A continuous video signal upon a tape (e.g. a television programme) used by **Linear Editing** systems to enable **Insert Editing**.

Coverage - A system of covering action within a scene with a standard selection of shots, such as a **Master**, **Singles**, and **Cutaways**.

Crabbing - Moving the camera sideways.

Cross-Fade - See **Dissolve**.

Crossing The Line - See **180° Rule**.

CU - Close-Up. A shot size showing most of the face.

Cutaway - A shot used in editing to cut away momentarily from the main action - perhaps the reaction of another character, or a simple physical action.

DAC - **D**igital to **A**nalogue **C**onverter. A device which encodes a **Digital** signal into an **Analogue** signal. Even if a camera or VCR is **Digital**, all outputs will be **Analogue** unless specifically labelled as **Digital**, for instance a **Firewire** connection. See **ADC**.

Daylight - Daylight has a **Colour Temperature** of approximately 5600° **Kelvin**, and appears blue if the camera is not correctly **White Balanced**. See also **Gels**.

Daylight Balanced Lights - A type of professional film light which has the same **Colour Temperature** as **Daylight**, either of the **HMI** or **MSR** type. About twice as efficient as **Tungsten** lights - therefore twice as powerful for the same wattage.

Depth Of Field - The depth of area which is in focus at any one time. Deeper on **Wide-Angle Lenses** than **Telephoto Lenses**. Made greater by closing down the **Aperture/Iris**.

Diffuser - Anything which softens light, such as **Trace**, smoke machines, Promist **Filters**, some **Reflectors** etc. See **Soft Light** and **Hard Light**.

Digital - Any device which records or uses video or audio information as a series of noughts and ones, as opposed to **Analogue**. If video or audio is copied digitally (**Cloned**), it suffers no **Generation Loss**.

Digitisation - The process of encoding video or audio information into computer files on **Non-Linear Editing** systems. Similar to 'sampling' in music.

Directional Microphone - A microphone designed to pick up sound from one direction only. See **Rifle Mike**.

Director of Photography (DoP) - Member of the crew responsible for lighting and camera-work.

Dissolve - A **Transition** from one shot to another in which the two pictures mix together. Aka **Cross-Fade**.

Dolly - A wheeled camera mounting which runs on tracks or rubber wheels.

Dubbing - Copying video or audio from one tape to another with an analogue component somewhere along the way which will result eventually in **Generation Loss**.

Dubbing Studio - A facility for the mixing of audio for film and television productions.

DV - **D**igital Video. Used confusingly to refer to one or all of the digital video formats - Mini-DV, DVCAM, DVCPro, Digital S, Betacam SX and Digital Betacam.

Dynamic Microphone - A microphone which uses a mechanical process to pick up sound, and is less fragile than a **Condenser Microphone**.

ECU - **E**xtreme **C**lose-**U**p. Used to refer to any extremely close shot, but in terms of the face, usually means a shot showing just the eyes.

Edit Controller - A device used in **Linear Editing** to issue commands to the VCRs.

EDL - **E**dit **D**ecision **L**ist. A text file created by a **Non-Linear Editing** system which contains basic information about an edit.

ELS - **E**xtremely **L**ong **S**hot. Any shot in which the subject is very small in **Frame**.

EQ - **EQ**ualisation. An audio control which adjusts the **Levels** of individual frequencies of sound.

Featured Music - aka **Incidental Music**. Music not heard by the characters in a scene.

Field - Half of a video **Frame**. Two of these are interleaved to make each frame. See **Film Look**.

Fill Light - A light (usually **Soft Light**) used to fill in shadows; an element of **Three-Point Lighting**.

Film Look - The process of making video look like film. Can involve doubling the **Fields** to mimic the frame rate of film, **Grading**, styles of lighting used during the shoot etc.

Filter - A glass plate, usually slotted in front of the lens in a **Matte Box**, which can cut the levels of light entering the lens (e.g. **Neutral Density**), act as a **Diffuser** (e.g. a Promist), change the **Colour Temperature** of incoming light (used only for film cameras) or add a cosmetic effect.

Firewire - A direct digital to digital audio/video connection with no **DAC** or **ADC** between the two machines.

First Assembly - The first complete edit of the film.

Flag - A large, flat object used to mask out unwanted light.

Flare - See **Lens Flare**.

Flood - Using the **Spot**/Flood control on a light to widen the beam of light, make it a little softer and a little less intense.

Fluorescent - A form of lighting which uses an electrically charged gas to emit light. Tends to cast a green tinge onto the subject, and therefore problematic - see **Gels**.

Focus Pulling - Changing focus during a shot.

Foley - Sound effects recorded in a studio during post-production, named after Jack Foley, who pioneered the technique. Aka **Footsteps** and **Spot Effects**.

Footsteps - See **Foley**.

FPS - Frames Per Second. The normal frame rate for **PAL** video is 25 fps. Film is normally shot at 24 fps.

Frame - A single picture of video or film (see **FPS**); the TV or film screen (see **Framing**).

Frameline - The edge of the frame in real space. Boom operators in particular must be aware of this.

Framing - The choices of shot size and contents of the screen.

Fresnel Lens - A lens used on professional lights to make them more directional and controllable.

Fullscreen - The 4:3 **aspect ratio** of a normal TV screen, known in cinema as Academy format.

Gaffer Tape - A form of adhesive tape (similar to duct tape) used extensively to hold productions together.

Gain - (Audio) The input **Level** control. (Video) A function on a video camera which electronically amplifies light levels; brightens the picture but adds grain.

Gels - Sheets of translucent plastic which affect the quality of light passing through them. Can be used to correct **Colour Temperature** or **Fluorescent** lights, control light levels (see **Neutral Density**) or add a cosmetic effect.

Generation Loss - A result of copying **Analogue** video or audio. Since the copy is not exact, interference is added with every new generation, eventually leading to the complete loss of the signal.

Genny - Common term for the generators used on larger shoots.

Gobo - An object used in lighting to cast a specific shadow and break up light, e.g. a tree branch.

Grading - The process of adjusting colour levels in footage to correct mistakes, improve continuity or add effects (such as a sepia tone). See **Colourisation**.

Green Room - An ante-room near to the set or studio where performers can relax.

Grip - A member of crew responsible for camera mountings like **Dollies** etc.

Hard Cut - A cut in which both sound and picture cut at the same time. Can be very obtrusive. See **Soft Cut**.

Hard Light - Directional light (e.g. from the sun or a naked light bulb) which throws harsh, well-defined shadows. See **Soft Light**, **Diffuser**.

Headroom - The space left between the top of the **Frame** and the head of a subject.

High Key - A style of lighting in which subjects and backgrounds are well-lit with primarily **Soft Light** (but which has no relation to the term **Key Light**). See also **Low Key**.

HMI - The older form of **Daylight Balanced Light**, cheaper but heavier.

Image Stabiliser - A device in small, lightweight video cameras which counters camera shake by either digital or optical means; optical is the better of the two.

Incidental Music - See **Featured Music**.

In Point - Programmable point at which an editing system will begin recording, digitising, playing etc.

Insert Editing - A form of **Linear Editing** which allows for shots to be dropped in at any point of a tape which has **Control Track** recorded on it.

Jack - A ¼" wide **Unbalanced** audio lead, which can carry either stereo or mono sound. Often used for headphones and in **Patch Bays**.

Jump Cut - A picture cut which goes to the same framing on a subject, but a subject which has changed position.

Kelvin - A measure of temperature in which the degrees are equivalent to those of Celsius/Centigrade, but which starts counting from absolute zero (-273.15°C).

Key Light - The main illumination on a subject, usually **Hard Light**; an element of **Three-Point Lighting**.

Lastolite - A **Reflector** consisting of reflective fabric stretched within a collapsible ring.

Lens Flare - A stray reflection of direct light hitting the lens at such an angle that a bright patch appears on the screen.

Letter-Box - A way of recording a **Widescreen** picture onto a **Fullscreen** picture which leaves black bars at the top and bottom of the screen but preserves the original **Aspect Ratio**.

Levels - The 'volume' at which incoming audio is recorded (the actual volume control affects the overall sound mix going out to speakers rather than sound coming in). Set with **Gain** control. See also **EQ**, **Compressor**.

Lighting Cameraman - The same as a **Director of Photography**, but the Lighting Cameraman operates the camera as well.

Linear Editing - Any editing system which works by recording video from one VCR to another. An inherent problem is that new material cannot be inserted earlier on the tape; it can only be copied over material already present. See **Scratch Editing**, **Assemble Editing**, **Insert Editing**, **2-Machine Suite**, **3-Machine Suite**, **Non-Linear Editing**.

Lines Off - Lines delivered off camera.

Logging - The process of compiling a list of what footage is on a tape. Often used to make a list of **Clips** for **Batch Digitising**.

Long Lens - See **Telephoto Lens**.

Looping - See **ADR**.

Low Key - A style of lighting which allows for a lot of shadows in frame and often uses **Hard Light** to throw some more (but which has no relation to the term **Key Light**). See also **High Key**.

LS - Long Shot. A shot size in which a human figure is shown from head to foot.

Mark - A marking on the floor (often done with **Gaffer Tape** or **Camera Tape**) which shows where an actor is at a specific point during their performance. Actors have to 'hit' their marks.

Master - A shot which encompasses the whole of the action within a scene.

Match Action - A cut which goes from one action to the same action, but seen from a different angle.

Matte Box - An apparatus on the front of a professional camera which both shields the lens from **Flare** and provides space to slot in **Filters**.

MCU - Medium Close-Up. A shot size encompassing the head and shoulders of a subject.

Memory Effect - The tendency of Nickel-Cadmium (NiCad) batteries to 'remember' the point at which they stopped charging, and to only charge to that point in future. Lithium-Ion (Li-Ion) batteries do not suffer from this.

Minijack - A miniature version of the **Jack**, also **Unbalanced** and capable of both stereo and mono. Commonly used for headphones. Some **DV** cameras have a version which carries video as well as both channels of audio.

MLS - Medium Long Shot. A shot size in which the subject is shown from the head to the knees.

Modelling - The effect created by lighting in which light and shade combine to bring out the depth of a subject; assisted by a combination of **Hard Light**, **Soft Light**, and **Back Light**.

Monitor - (Video) A small TV which is used to watch footage directly from the camera; any high-quality TV used in the production process. (Audio) The high-quality pair of speakers used in edit suites and **Dubbing Studios**.

Morticians' Wax - A putty-like substance which can be moulded to look like human skin; used in conjunction with make-up to create realistic wounds, scars etc.

MS - Medium Shot, or Mid-Shot. A shot size showing a subject from head to abdomen.

MSR - The newer form of **Daylight Balanced Light**, more expensive but lighter.

Neutral Density - A kind of **Filter** or **Gel** which reduces the level of light passing through it.

Negative Bounce - Using a dark surface to absorb light instead of reflect it.

Noise Gate - An effects box in a **Dubbing Studio** which can be set to only allow sound through above a certain volume, e.g. it can be used to cut out background noise in-between the words spoken by a performer.

Non-Linear Editing - Any form of editing system with the capability to insert ('splice in') footage at any point in the edit, pushing aside that which was there before. Applies to film editing as well as computer-based systems. See **Digitisation**, **Batch Digitising**, **Timeline**, **Bin**, **Clip**, **Project**, **Linear Editing**.

NTSC - The American/Japanese/Canadian television standard, incompatible with **PAL** and **SECAM**. Runs at a frame rate of 29.97 or 30 fps. Too hideously complex for words.

Offline - The rough edit of a video. On **Linear Editing** systems, the offline is the rough stage before the **Online** stage, which can be on almost any video format, usually the cheapest. On **Non-Linear Editing** systems, an edit made with lower-quality (more compressed) footage prior to the **Online**.

Online - The final edit of a video. On **Linear Editing** systems, this is done on the highest quality video format available, and **Grading**, titles and other video effects are added. In **Non-Linear Editing** systems, these may already have been done, leaving only the redigitisation of footage at higher quality, possibly on the same system.

Out Point - Programmable point at which an editing system will stop recording, digitising, playing etc.

Outline - A rough working out of the plot of a story, sometimes done on index cards.

PAL - TV standard adopted in the UK, incompatible with **NTSC** and **SECAM**. Runs at 25 fps.

Pan and Scan - The system used to transfer most **Widescreen** films to video, in which the sides of the frame are cut off, but the TV screen 'pans' across the frame if it needs to.

Pan - (Camera) Turning the camera left or right. (Audio) Moving the perceived position of sound between two stereo speakers.

Paper Edit - A rough edit of the film done on paper.

Patch Bay - A system of sending video or audio signals between a number of pieces of equipment. Outputs and inputs for each bit of kit are all plugged into a line of sockets which can then be connected with patch leads.

Phantom Power - Power supplied to a **Condenser Microphone**. Can come from a sound desk or through batteries.

Phase Converter - A device which matches the frame rate of a TV or computer monitor to that of the camera.

Phono - An **Unbalanced** lead that can carry one channel of audio or video.

Pick-Up - A shot to be filmed separately from the rest, usually something that was over-looked in the original schedule or discovered during editing.

Picture Lock - The point during editing at which the picture edit is completed, and locked down before the film goes to a sound mix at a **Dubbing Studio**.

Playback - Audio playing facilities on set, usually used to play music so performers have something to dance to.

Polecat - A type of lighting stand which has rubber feet at both ends and is extendible to allow it to be wedged between any two surfaces.

Polyboard - A sheet of polystyrene, used as a **Reflector**, or, when painted black, for **Negative Bounce**.

Post-Production - The stage of a project after shooting, when the film is edited, music is composed & recorded and sound is mixed.

POV - Point Of View. A shot which is seen as though through the eyes of a character.

Practical - Used to describe any prop or item on screen which actually works; also used to describe a light in vision which is used as part of the lighting set-up, as opposed to most ordinary lights, which are too dull for film and television.

Pre-Production - Stage of a project in which the shoot is planned and prepared.

Preroll - The amount of time a VCR will run backwards to before the **In-Point** and then start playing.

Preview - A function of **Linear Editing** systems which allows a cut to be checked before it is made.

Production - The shoot of the film or video.

Project - Term used to refer to a complete set of **Bins**, **Clips**, **Timeline** etc. on a **Non-Linear Editing** system.

Redhead - A 800 watt **Tungsten** light without a **Fresnel** lens.

Reflector - Any surface used to bounce light, such as walls, **Polyboards**, **Lastolites** etc. A silvery surface reflects **Hard Light** while a light-coloured matt surface reflects **Soft Light**.

Rendering - The calculations made by a **Non-Linear Editing** system to add effects to digitised footage.

Repeat - (Audio) A repeated or reflected sound, such as an echo. (Props & Costumes) A replacement item identical to another which must be destroyed or soiled during a take.

Reverb - The continuous reflections of sound that come from hard surfaces in an enclosed area, which seem to make a sound continue on; the effects box which recreates this in a **Dubbing Studio**.

Rifle Mike - A particularly **Directional Microphone** often mounted on a **Boom**.

Room Tone - See **Atmos**.

Safety - An extra take made just in case all the previous takes were faulty in some way.

SCART - Standard European AV connector, often used on consumer TVs and VCRs.

Scratch Editing - The process of **Linear Editing** with a system which can be put together from ordinary consumer equipment.

Scrim - Perforated sheet clipped to **Barn Doors** (like **Gels** or **Trace**) in order to cut down light.

Script Supervisor - Member of crew responsible for continuity.

SECAM - TV standard used in France and the former Soviet Union (among others). Incompatible with **PAL** and **NTSC**.

Set Dressing - Anything in shot on a set which is there for design purposes rather than to be used as a prop (although it's nice if it can be used - if it is **Practical** - just in case).

Shoot Ratio - The ratio between the length of the film and the length of footage actually shot.

Showreel - A short video containing previous work of an individual or organisation.

Shutter - The device within a camera which opens to allow light through one time for each frame. The longer it is open, the more blurred movement will be within the frame.

Single - A shot on one character within a scene.

Slate - Common term for a **Clapperboard**.

Slugline - The location description line in a script e.g. INT. CABINET ROOM - DAY.

Soft Cut - A cut which staggers the cutting of picture and sound; assists continuity and masks the unnaturalness of the cut. See **Hard Cut**.

Soft Light - Non-directional light which radiates in a kind of glow. It casts a less distinct shadow than **Hard Light** and is created by using a **Diffuser**.

Sound Mixer - A device used on location to mix incoming sound and set levels before sending it to a recording device (usually either the camera or a **DAT**), often called an **SQN**.

Spark - An electrician.

Special FX - Environmental effects such as snow, wind, rain, smoke etc.

Splicing - The action of physically cutting film and putting it back together; an equivalent operation performed by a **Non-Linear Editing** system.

Spot - Using the Spot/**Flood** control on a light to narrow the beam of light, make it a little harder and a little more intense.

Spot Effects - See **Foley**.

SQN - See **Sound Mixer**.

Steadicam - A camera mounting which rests upon an operator and keeps the camera steady while the operator is able to move around.

Storyboard - A sequence of drawings used to plan what shots will be required for a film.

Subtext - Meaning which is implied but not directly revealed. The implication can be created by performance or by information already given to the audience.

S-Video - A type of video cable associated with the S-VHS format but now found on many cameras and VCRs.

Sync Sound - Sound recorded in sync with the picture. See also **Wildtrack**, **Clapperboard**.

Telephoto Lens - Commonly known as a **Long Lens**. Includes less of the picture in the frame, making the subject seem nearer. Gives a flatter picture and has a narrow **Depth of Field**. See also **Wide-Angle Lens** and **Zoom Lens**.

Temp Music - Music used during editing in place of music to be composed later.

Three-Point Lighting - A textbook system of lighting mainly used for interviews but containing the basic ideas that go towards lighting in general. The three points are three lights: **Key Light**, **Fill Light** and **Back Light**.

Tilt - Tilting the camera up and down on a tripod or other camera mounting.

Timecode - A frame-by-frame numbering system, encoded alongside video information or between frames. Appears in the format HH:MM:SS:FF. See also **BITC**.

Timeline - The part of a **Non-Linear Editing** system which graphically shows the edit as a timeline composed of video and audio tracks.

Trace - A type of fireproof paper used as **Diffuser** by pegging it onto the **Barn Doors** of a light.

Tracking - A smooth form of camera movement using a **Dolly**, which may or may not actually be on tracks.

Transition - Any movement between two shots which is not a simple cut, such as a **Cross-Fade** or a **Wipe**.

Treatment - A telling of the story used as a selling document. Actual definitions of the content of a treatment vary enormously.

Tungsten - Tungsten lights have a **Colour Temperature** of approximately 3200° **Kelvin**, and appear orange if the camera is not correctly **White Balanced**. See also **Gels**.

Unbalanced - See **Balanced**.

Video Mixer - A device used in **Linear Editing** suites which can mix video signals and add video effects.

Vignetting - Used to refer to a **Frame** which has the edge of the lens in shot.

Visual FX - Almost any effects work including prosthetics, animatronics, CGI etc. but excluding environmental effects (see **Special FX**).

White Balance - A control on most cameras which adjusts to match the **Colour Temperature** of light. See also **Daylight** and **Tungsten**.

Wide-Angle Lens - Includes more of the picture in the frame, making the subject seem further away, but, in extreme cases, makes nearer objects bulge towards the screen. Gives a more three-dimensional look and has a large **Depth of Field**. See also **Telephoto Lens** and **Zoom Lens**.

Widescreen - Any film or video frame with an **Aspect Ratio** wider than 4:3 (**Fullscreen**). Widescreen TVs are 16:9, but cinema films are usually either 1.85:1 or 2.35:1.

Wildtrack - Any sound recorded 'wild', i.e. not with picture. Generally used to refer to sound effects recorded on location.

Wipe - A form of **Transition** in which one picture replaces another by 'wiping' across it.

Wrap - When work at a location is finished, the work of packing up equipment and getting out; also, the very end of the shoot.

XLR - A **Balanced** audio lead. Aka **Cannon**.

Zoom Lens - A lens standard on most video cameras which allows the user to 'zoom' in on a subject, making it seem apparently closer on the screen. Effectively, the zoom lens is both a **Wide-Angle Lens** and a **Telephoto Lens** (though not at the extremes of either); zooming in or out changes the properties of the lens from one to the other.

The Essential Library

New: **Filming On A Microbudget** by Paul Hardy (£3.99)
Terry Pratchett by Andrew M Butler (£3.99)
The Hitchhiker's Guide by M J Simpson (£3.99)

Film: **Woody Allen** by Martin Fitzgerald (£2.99)
Jane Campion by Ellen Cheshire (£2.99)
John Carpenter by Colin Odell & Michelle Le Blanc (£3.99)
Jackie Chan by Michelle Le Blanc & Colin Odell (£2.99)
Joel & Ethan Coen by John Ashbrook & Ellen Cheshire (£2.99)
David Cronenberg by John Costello (£3.99)
Film Noir by Paul Duncan (£2.99)
Terry Gilliam by John Ashbrook (£2.99)
Heroic Bloodshed edited by Martin Fitzgerald (£2.99)
Alfred Hitchcock by Paul Duncan (£2.99)
Horror Films by Colin Odell & Michelle Le Blanc (£3.99)
Krzysztof Kieslowski by Monika Maurer (£2.99)
Stanley Kubrick by Paul Duncan (£2.99)
David Lynch by Michelle Le Blanc & Colin Odell (£3.99)
Steve McQueen by Richard Luck (£2.99)
Marilyn Monroe by Paul Donnelley (£3.99)
The Oscars® by John Atkinson (£3.99)
Brian De Palma by John Ashbrook (£2.99)
Sam Peckinpah by Richard Luck (£2.99)
Ridley Scott by Brian J Robb (£3.99)
Slasher Movies by Mark Whitehead (£3.99)
Vampire Films by Michelle Le Blanc & Colin Odell (£2.99)
Orson Welles by Martin Fitzgerald (£2.99)
Billy Wilder by Glenn Hopp (£3.99)

TV: **Doctor Who** by Mark Campbell (£3.99)

Books: **Cyberpunk** by Andrew M Butler (£3.99)
Philip K Dick by Andrew M Butler (£3.99)
Noir Fiction by Paul Duncan (£2.99)

Culture:**Conspiracy Theories** by Robin Ramsay (£3.99)

Available at all good bookstores, or send a cheque to: **Pocket Essentials (Dept FMB), 18 Coleswood Rd, Harpenden, Herts, AL5 1EQ, UK**. Please make cheques payable to 'Oldcastle Books.' Add 50p postage & packing for each book in the UK and £1 elsewhere.

US customers can send $6.95 plus $1.95 postage & packing for each book to: **Trafalgar Square Publishing, PO Box 257, Howe Hill Road, North Pomfret, Vermont 05053, USA**. e-mail: tsquare@sover.net

Customers worldwide can order online at **www.pocketessentials.com**.

The Christmas Story

Published by Evans Brothers Ltd
2A Portman Mansions
Chiltern St
London W1U 6NR

This edition first published 2003

The text of The Christmas Story is based on The Birth
of Jesus, one of nine stories first published in Christian
Stories, a title in the Storyteller series published by
Evans Brothers Ltd.

British Library Cataloguing in Publication Data
Ganeri, Anita
        The Christmas story
        1. Jesus Christ – Nativity
        I. Title II. Phillips, Rachel
        232.9'2

ISBN 0 237 524686

Printed in Hong Kong by Wing King Tong Co. Ltd

Editor: Louise John
Designer: Simon Borrough
Illustrations: Rachael Phillips, Allied Artists
Production: Jenny Mulvanny
Consultants: Father Martin Robindra Ganeri O.P.
Alan Brown

Acknowledgements
For permission to reproduce copyright material, the
author and publishers gratefully acknowledge the
following:
page 20 Trip/H Rogers
page 21 the art archive

THE Christmas Story

Anita Ganeri

Illustrated by
Rachael Phillips

EVANS BROTHERS LIMITED